I0470597

Building Manufacturing Competitiveness

Competitiveness

The TOC Way

Building Manufacturing Competitiveness

Competitiveness

The TOC Way

Shridhar Lolla, PhD

Building Manufacturing Competiveness - the TOC Way

Copyrights © Shridhar Lolla 2013

All rights reserved. This book or any portion thereof may not be reproduced or used in any manner whatsoever without the express written permission of the publisher.

Edition 1: 2012, Edition 2.1: 2013

ISBN-10: 1484198727

ISBN-13: 978-1484198728

Keywords: *Manufacturing, Production, Operations, Product Development, Productivity, Continuous Improvement, Sustainable Growth, Operational Excellence, Operational Management, Theory of Constraints, TOC, Constraint Management, Time Management*

Published by Shridhar Lolla
#2304, Nandi Park, Gottigere
Bannergatta Road, Bangalore- 560 083
INDIA
E mail: lolla@cvmark.com

The Book is based on the experience of the Author. The names, characters, dates and places used in the Book are fictional and any resemblance to reality is purely coincidental. The Book also contains information that might seem prescriptive in nature. The Author can't assume any responsibility for the validity of all the materials or consequence of their use. The Author has attempted to trace the copyright holders of materials reproduced in this publication and apologize to copyright holders if permission to publish in this form has not been obtained. If any copyright material has not been acknowledged please write and let him know so he may rectify in any further reprint.

Trademark Notice: Product or corporate names may be trademarks or registered trademarks, and are used only for identification and explanation without intent to infringe.

To those who are firefighting,
As they remain busy pushing thing
To fulfill their promise to customers,
And wonder
When will the grind halt,
When will the flow smoothen and
When will life be fulfilling...

I saw them in Steel Mills,
I was with them in Factories,
I lived with them in Offices...
It is time,
Life comes to them.

Preface

The United States is pursuing an elaborate plan to reclaim its manufacturing dominance. Several other countries including the UK, Germany, Brazil and India too are increasing investment to strengthen their manufacturing base. In fact, the world over, countries are betting their next decade of growth on the competitiveness of their manufacturing sector.

However, the current business environment has become ever more complex and chaotic, necessitating manufacturing organizations to not only make radical improvement in their performance, but also make such improvements faster. Supported by respective national manufacturing policies, organizations are therefore, bracing to dramatically and quickly lift their performance levels, while simultaneously guaranteeing high quality and competitive prices.

There are several, rather too many techniques in the world which can be used to improve some or other aspect of manufacturing organizations. However, sustained improvement seems to require enormous amount of effort, time and cost. Attempts made by several organizations to pick one technique or the other to improve performance have often given unsatisfactory results. Also, when the competition is ever fiercer, the days of sustaining on small incremental benefits are often found lost in the noise.

Today, organizations need a mechanism that allows them to obtain significant benefits quickly without taking too much of risk and without exhausting scarce resources. And such a mechanism must suit to their local and regional settings.

When there is so much complexity and chaos around, focusing on right things is the right approach. Theory of Constraints, TOC as propounded by Eliyahu Goldratt, offers a proven mechanism for organizations to achieve an order of magnitude of growth quickly with minimum effort, cost and risk. Further, the approach is intuitive and harmonious for organizational transformation.

This book, *Building Manufacturing Competitiveness - the TOC Way*, exposes application of TOC to manufacturing organizations. It picks up the context of India to highlight how application of TOC can be dovetailed to its national agenda to dramatically improve manufacturing competitiveness. An Indian context seems very relevant, since India has been at the forefront of global economic growth. However, the events of 2008-2012 have confirmed that low GDP share of India's manufacturing sector could prevent it from sustaining the past high level of growth. India is now aggressively building competitiveness of its manufacturing industry. In fact, by 2022, it targets to improve share of its Manufacturing GDP from 16% to 25% and generate 100 million new jobs.

The book considers two key areas in manufacturing organizations, namely Production and Product Development, and showcases how application of TOC builds a *reinforcing effect* between them to drive quick and significant business growth on an ongoing basis. By doing so, the book intends to guide manufacturing sector in achieving sustainable growth in today's hyper competitive world.

Although, TOC was first employed over 25 years back in solving business problems, only during the last decade it gained momentum in India. Thanks to its growing body of knowledge, an increasing number of Indian organizations are showing interest in implementing TOC concepts in their operations. In fact, India now has one of the largest groups of TOC experts. It looks natural, therefore, that the potential of TOC is linked to a larger agenda. India's growing thrust on dramatically improving its manufacturing GDP offers an opportunity to take advantage of TOC as an operational improvement framework for its manufacturing industry. However, despite the growing adoption of TOC in India, availability of a single source of reference linking application of TOC to India's need and environment has been lacking. This book tries to fill the gap.

The book is laid into four themes. The first theme is about India's manufacturing agenda and it brings out the urgency to improve performance of its industries. The second theme is about application of TOC in dramatically and quickly improving performance of manufacturing organizations. The third theme relates to the realm of TOC and its status in India.

When such a profound concept is presented, often we are asked a question, "Where do we start?" The fourth theme of the book is, therefore, about three case based hints on where and how to start a TOC initiative.

I hope that the attempt to link methodologies of TOC in a national context, make the book informative, interesting and useful to the practitioners, experts and academics alike.

Shridhar Lolla   2013, Bangalore, India

Contents

An Urgent Agenda for the Industry

The Objective

The objective of the book is to propose an approach to build breakthrough competitiveness in Indian Manufacturing Companies. The book intends to take organizations on the path of rapidly implementing their strategies to increase revenues and sales through a superlative operational performance.

Since, time is the biggest constraint and competition is ever fiercer, organizations need to master responsiveness as their key weapon and be ahead in the race. However, a higher degree of responsiveness in an ever changing business conditions can only be achieved with a focused approach in delivering what the market demands. Such a focused approach must take cognizance of India's natural settings and therefore, leverage the existing investment made by the organizations and their human capital, without taking too much of risk and without exhausting costly resources.

The book presents Theory of Constraints, TOC as a focusing mechanism to offer Indian Manufacturing Companies an approach to build world class competitiveness. TOC, being a proven methodology, recognizes aspects of today's external and internal requirements, and provides a direction to organizations in rapidly building a sustainable operating culture of excellence.

The Manufacturing Thrust at National Level

During the last two decades, Indian economy achieved significant growth. It is now well established that the growth was largely driven by the high skill service sector.

It was also said that India had leapfrogged from agriculture to service sector. It is now realized that the said growth was obtained at the neglect of manufacturing and agriculture sectors. And the progress has not been enough to provide equitable growth including employment opportunities for the majority of India's working age population, a vast majority of which is less than middle school educated.

With the experience of the past, the logic for future growth of India is becoming clearer day by day. For India to grow, it must allow seamless flow of growth across its three sectors.

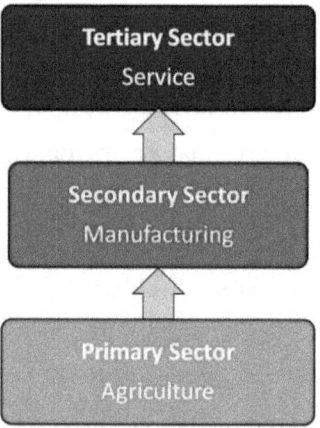

Figure 1.1 Sectoral Classification of the Economy

First, India must be self sufficient in its food supplies, which means that agricultural produce must be available in abundance, accessible across the country and affordable to all. It means that agriculture industry must be highly productive. Today, with over 60% of the working population being agrarian, the per capita productivity of Indian agriculture is too low to allow the overall economy deliver high growth levels. The agricultural productivity therefore, must improve dramatically, for which it needs to improve efficiency of its processes across the value chain. As a consequence, it means that a huge working population would move out of agriculture sector.

Now, since a vast majority of the working age population of India is sub middle school educated, it can't be absorbed in the high skill service sector easily. Hence, for considerably long time in future, India would look up to its manufacturing sector for employment. Thus, the present stage of development of India dictates that manufacturing sector shoulders the responsibility of creating equitable growth and jobs.

In fact, the current stage of maturity of the Indian economy also means that the growth of the service sector is also dependent on the growth of manufacturing sector (manufacturing sector has significant multiplier effect on growth of service sector). Thus, under the sectoral classification of Indian economy, manufacturing sector has become the Bottleneck. That is, a sustainable growth of Indian economy is *limited* by the growth of its manufacturing sector (Remember, a bottleneck decides the flow of liquid out of the bottle. Similarly, for today's Indian Economy, its manufacturing sector decides the overall growth of the nation.)

So, as productivity of agriculture improves and more rural population turns to urban areas for better quality of life, the real challenge India faces is how it could keep up its GDP growth, while most of its working population concentrates in manufacturing sector. The only way India can give its vast population a higher quality of life and a sustained GDP growth is by increasing its manufacturing GDP dramatically.

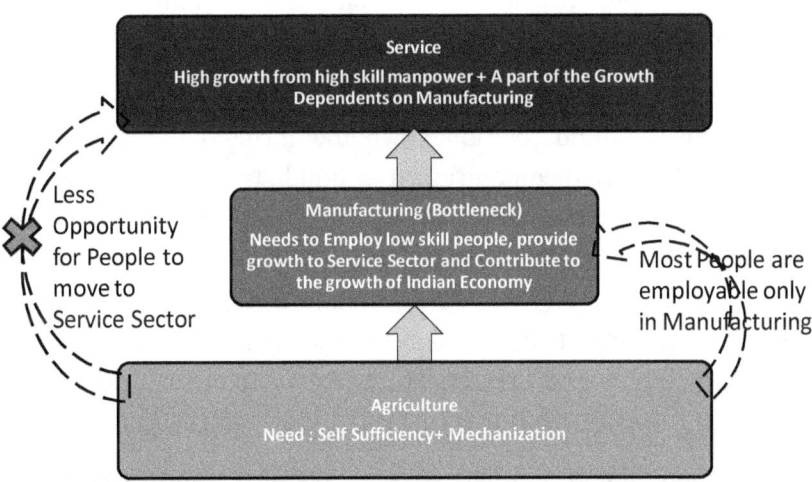

Figure 1.2 Manufacturing Sector is the bottleneck in the growth of Indian Economy

An Approach to Increase Manufacturing GDP

There is the usual way of increasing manufacturing GDP: make investment in factories and infrastructure. However, it means huge capital outlay, efforts and long gestation period. This is the first step when the asking rate is high and there is a need to provide equitable growth. In the language of management science, this type of growth is called investment based growth, which is complex, long term and often, for a resource limited country, difficult to fund internally. This approach, not avoidable for the current stage of manufacturing sector of India, can give scale and deploy new manufacturing technology, but may not guarantee a sustainable manufacturing competitiveness.

Given that time is the key constraint for achieving a globally competitive position, the only way manufacturing sector can become competitive without taking too much risk and without exhausting costly national resources, is by improving productivity across the shop floors of manufacturing organizations. Ultimately, *global competitiveness means how much of GDP contribution comes from per capita working population* and not just the gross GDP. Higher productivity per capita means more volume, more variety, better quality and lower cost, all together. The challenge of productivity improvement is so much more daunting for India because so many people would be moving to manufacturing sector and their initial productivity levels would not be very high.

Keeping this in mind, National Manufacturing Competitiveness Council, NMCC has been entrusted to build strategy for providing the next level of growth in India from manufacturing sector. India now has a Manufacturing Strategy, and it has come out with a New Manufacturing Policy (NMP) that intends to take contribution of manufacturing sector from 16 % of GDP in 2012 to 25% within 10 years, i.e. by 2022. And in doing so, it intends to create 100 million new jobs.

Several structural and regulatory issues have been addressed in the NMP to bring huge investment into manufacturing sector. The *ultimate game of competitiveness* will, however, be played by productivity levels of the nation at the firm and individual level. Alas! Such competitiveness will not be achieved merely by the economy of scale quickly and without exhausting costly resources. The NMP recognizes that compared to the global average, India lags in productivity levels by multiple fractions. It has therefore set its sight on aggressively rolling out programs to handhold Indian industries in building world class competitiveness.

It is not that Indian Manufacturing Industry does not use modern techniques of production and management. However, at the level of a firm, the approach is often a quick fix of one machine here and one technology there. Or it is building a plant here and acquiring another there. These pick and choose approaches do not readily build sustainable competitive edge, though may help in coming out of smaller crisis or taking advantage of the few opportunities.

The key to sustainable competitiveness of Indian manufacturing organizations would depend on an ongoing process of excellence. For which they must build the way to offer a *variety* of *quality products* to the global market at a *speed and cost* that is unmatched elsewhere.

The Challenge in Manufacturing at Organization Level

At the level of a Firm, an organization seeks to move towards its goal of making money today as well as tomorrow. While it tries to move towards its goal, at each step, it finds the environment within and outside changing rapidly and unpredictably. Also since at the level of the firm, resources are highly constrained, under an ever changing environment doing justice with near term goals and long term objective becomes complex.

There is a saying that when the change is rampant one must have the ability to change faster than the change. Control System Engineers and Change Managers know that under such a situation, it is important to do a faster sampling of the output and the environment, and build an even faster responsive system. In business too, in order to be competitive, it is imperative that *organizations become more responsive in dealing with rapidly changing and frequently unpredictable business environment.*

Responsive Operations

Within an organizational setup, a significant degree of responsiveness or the 'rate' of delivering value to customers is provided by a function or process called 'Operations'. The competitive challenge at the level of a firm therefore boils down to achieving Responsive Operations that is aligned to its long term objective of sustainable growth.

The operational responsiveness of an organization is measured in terms of Lead Time and On Time Delivery (OTD) with respect to the promise made to the market. These two metrics hold the key to competitive positioning and therefore, organizations must strive to ever shrink Lead Time, while improving OTD. And these must be achieved at minimum cost and acceptable quality levels. An inevitable outcome of such a performance is dramatic improvement in throughput and productivity.

Rapid Product Development

While the day to day customer orders (process orders) form the basis of making money NOW, the growth of an organization in FUTURE is guaranteed only by new products brought into the market. It is, therefore, necessary that an organization brings out ever wider range of competitive products to the market.

Today, the innovation world is so open that the product development cycles are crashing dramatically. *Time to market has, therefore, become an important competitive metric and shorter time to market is now an imperative for Product Development.* The speed with which an organization brings out its products decides the leverage it has in tapping the market as an early mover.

The Dual Competitive Edge

Thus, in order to move closer to its overall goal of making money NOW, as well as in FUTURE, a manufacturing organization has two key performance metrics.

> 1. Fulfill day to day process orders *faster and on-time* despite all the reasonable near term variability and uncertainty. This, it delivers through a superlative Manufacturing Operational capabilities, for which having a responsive Production is a sub-objective.
> 2. Bring an ever wider range of new products *faster and in time* to the market. This, it achieves by building a superlative Product Development capabilities for which having a responsive project management capability is a sub-objective.

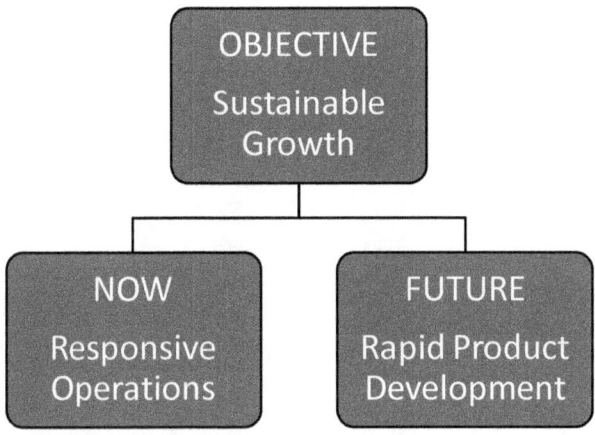

Figure 1.3 A Manufacturing organization must achieve responsiveness in both Operations and Product Development

The above two sub-objectives must be obtained without taking too much risk and without exhausting costly and scarce resources of the organization.

Responsive Production System

The Role of a Production System

A Production System is the key constituent of Operations in a manufacturing organization, which creates the key value offered by the organization. For Operations of an organization to be responsive, it has to be backed by a responsive Production System.

Traditionally, the objective of a Production System has been to achieve the highest possible throughput based on a forecasted demand.

However, under the current business environment, the market demands the production system to meet rapid and often unpredictable changes in scale (amount) and scope (variant) of products. For example, in a Made to Stock environment, the products planned today for production based on quarterly forecasting become slow moving even before they move to Finished Goods (FG) warehouse. At the same time, what is not forecasted today gets urgent takers very soon. Thus, organizations often face the problem of producing goods that get overstocked, while not producing goods that are in demand and are stocked out or delayed. Massive mismatches in supply and demand has been a part of production folklore.

For an organization, Throughput is no more just a quantitative metric, as the goods produced have meaning only if they are readily saleable (converted into money). This makes sense because in an ever changing and unpredictable business environment, maintaining a healthy cash flow is the top most organizational agenda of the organization.

It is therefore imperative that under current business environment, a Production System is highly responsive and flexible by design so that it can deal with the changes taking place in the market place. Faster the response (Lead Time), closer the production to meet the market demand and hence, less mismatches in the supply chain and less money locked in the system.

Figure 2.1 illustrates, typical situation of how mismatches happen in a made to stock environment. It shows that the shop floor is flooded with orders for product B and D (which are already full stock in the warehouse) instead of product A and B (which are on the verge of being stock out).

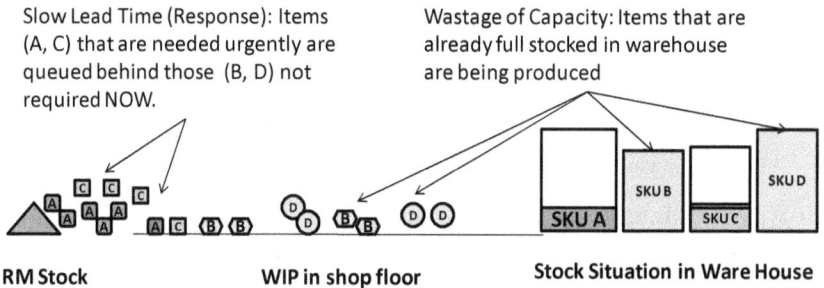

Figure 2.1 Producing what is not required NOW delays what is required NOW, and elongates the response time of the Production System

The Direction of Production

Translation of the above fundamental aspect into shop floor (production area) language means that a Production System not only has a scalar objective (how much) but also a direction (what to produce and when). Conversely, a Production System must know when not to waste its capacity on goods that are not required in near term.

It means that a Production System must have a mechanism to process only those work orders that are required by the market NOW (or in very short term), and must not process those not required NOW. Producing what is not required NOW instead of producing what is required NOW, only delays the response time to deliver what is required in the market NOW.

By having a mechanism to not waste capacity on making things that are not required NOW and working on things that are required NOW, a Production System not only improves its OTD, it also improves its response time by avoiding chaos and bloated work in progress. How do we design such a system?

What to Produce

For competitive products, the tolerance time of the market is usually significantly shorter than the production lead time (counted from the order receipt to delivery of goods). If an organization is in a competitive product market e.g. running brands of automobiles, consumer goods, fast moving industrial goods, commodities, etc. then its products must be available in stock before it receives customer order. That is, the products must be Made to Availability, MTA. However it is not advisable to just produce goods at will or on long forecasted cycle and stock them, otherwise it would lead to wastage of critical capacity, massive mismatches and sluggish response time.

Instead, as the products are consumed by the market from the stock, process orders are placed on the Production System. Under such a situation, replacement order is the only mechanism to raise process orders for production. Therefore, for Made to Availability products, production must avoid working on any orders other than those raised for replenishing the consumed stocks.

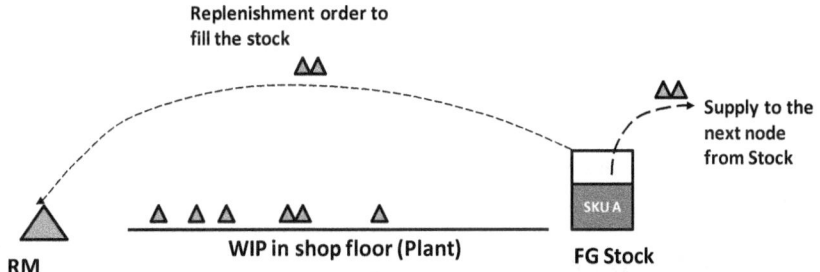

Figure 2.2 In a Make To Availability environment, orders released to the shop floor are only those for replenishing the depleted stock.

However, there are non competitive, made to engineer or customized products like heavy machinery, defense equipment, new products, etc. where the tolerance time of market is significantly longer than a typical production lead time. But these products must be delivered to customers as per a promised Due Date. In such cases, it does not make sense to keep stocks of these products pre-manufactured. An organization working on Make to Order (MTO) products must produce goods only based upon firm orders and should avoid producing any product that does not have a confirmed order.

Table 2.1 In Make To Order (MTO) environment, each order has a Due Date

Customer Order	Due Date
Order 9A12-004	20-Apr-2012
Order 9A12-005	30 Apr-2012
Order 9A12-006	02-May-2012
Order 9A12-007	08-May-2012
Order 9A12-008	15-May-2012
Order 9A12-009	30-May-2012

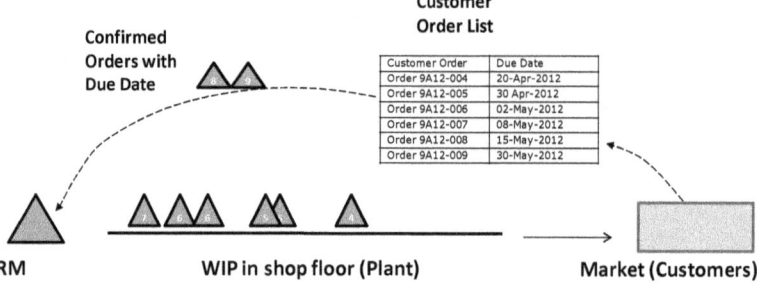

Figure 2.3 In Make to Order environment, the process orders released into the Production System are only due to firm orders and each order has a confirmed due date

When to Produce

While the system is set to know what to produce and what not to, often there are more products and orders to be processed than the number of available resources. And, there is a day to day conflict about which order to be processed first. Having multiple priorities based on preferences of individuals and events only compounds the confusion and chaos in the shop floor.

Based upon day to day supply-demand situation, some products (orders) have higher urgency than other products (orders). The system must have a mechanism to avoid working out an order that is less important and urgent than an order that is more important and urgent. For which, the system must be designed to identify higher priority orders from lower priority orders quickly and allocate resources accordingly. Doing this in a timely manner improves the promise made to the market (Availability, OTD and Lead Time).

In order to achieve such a flexibility, the system must operate with a single priority system - A priority system that helps in meeting a distinctive promise (Availability, OTD and Lead Time) made to customers, is a good priority system.

For MTA environment, to be competitive in the market, an organization makes an offer of 'high availability', i.e. it promises to make its products available in reasonably short lead time that is closer to transportation time. Such an organization must avoid a situation of stock out because stock out situation is an indication of immediate possible non-availability of stock, immediate loss of sales and failure to fulfill promise made to customers.

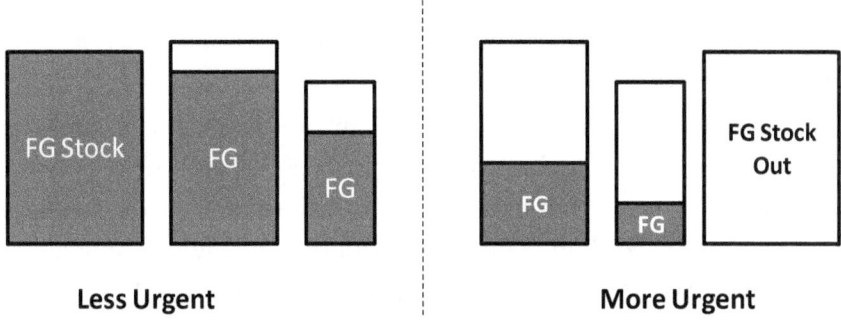

Less Urgent   **More Urgent**

Figure 2.4 For MTA products, a single Priority System could be based on urgency to avoid stock-out situation

Since organizations produce multiple products, on an ongoing basis different products are consumed at different rates. It means that different products fall into the danger of being stocked out at different times. An organization offering MTA products, therefore, needs a priority system that at any time provides highest for processing the products that are left with relatively least stock in hand, Figure 2.4.

Similarly, in the case of an MTO environment, an organization needs to set a single priority system that tells which order to be processed higher on priority given the situation of limited resources. At a given resource, the percentage of lead time left for an order to fulfill is often considered as the parameter for setting priority of MTO products, Figure 2.5.

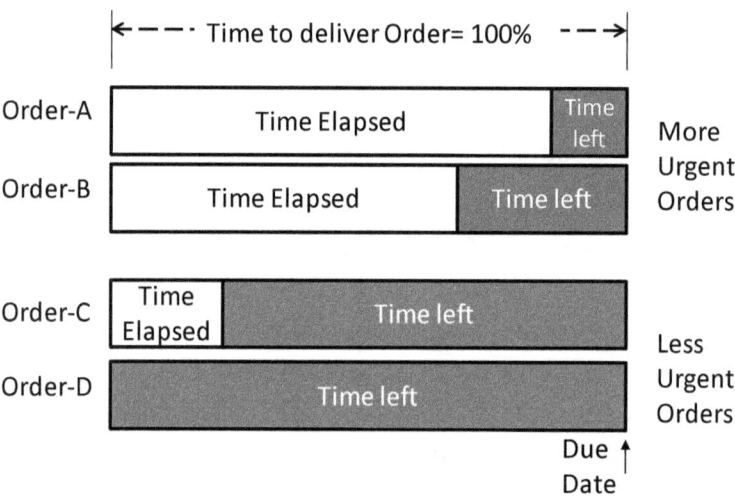

Figure 2.5 For MTO products, a Single Priority System could be based on urgency to avoid missing the promised Due Date

Classifying the desired level of System Stocks for MTA and the Production Lead Time for MTO into three zones of priority (Figure 2.6 and 2.7), provides a neutral way of prioritizing process orders in a Production System. At a given resource, the highest urgency is given to those orders that have least stocks or least time to due date (Red Zone).

Some production environments operate both MTA and MTO orders, under such a situation, the single color priority system based on urgency provides a neutral, common and unambiguous priority system for all products.

Of course, a smart Production System must operate with minimum urgencies, though severe urgencies due to spiked orders and sometimes due to Murphy and Black Swan Effect can't be avoided completely.

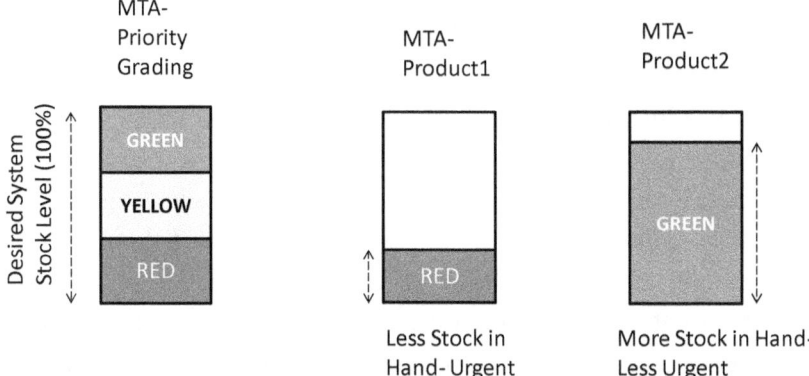

Figure 2.6 Color Based Priority System: for MTA products, Lower the Stock in Hand, Higher the Urgency (Priority)

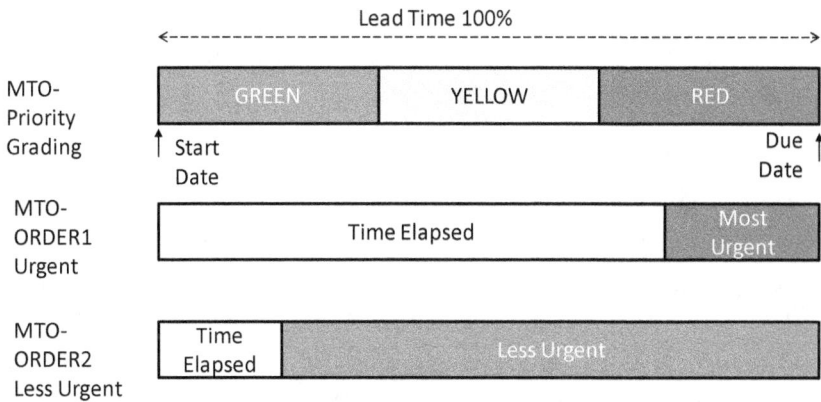

Figure 2.7 Color Based Priority System, for MTO Products, Shorter the Time Left for Due Date, Higher the Urgency (Priority)

As the Production System is aligned with the direction of the near term market demand, what it produces is sold in near term with low inventory. Its overstocks and stock-out problems reduce dramatically, while simultaneously its OTD improves and Lead Time shrinks. And its ability to respond to changes in demand also improves.

Improving Production - the TOC Way

Once a Production System aligns itself with the market demand and follows the discipline of not producing what is not required, it would reach high level of effectiveness. However in due course of time, the average demand on the Production System would increase and flow blockers will emerge. Also, the Production System will struggle to increase its capacity. It would then require more than a conscious effort to seek 'improvement' in the performance.

In fact, it is said that improvement is continuous and the prime role of a Production System is therefore, to ever improve the rate of flow of goods and services that are saleable in the near horizon of time. it is important to remember here is that the flow has both magnitude (throughput) as well as direction (product variety).

Various techniques and tools of continuous improvement have been used successfully in several organizations. 5S, SPC, Kanban, SMED, Poka Yoke, Lean, Six Sigma, TQM, Agile Manufacturing, MRP, ERP, Digitization, Automation, Outsourcing, Vendor Managed Inventory etc., provide specific tools and techniques to improve different parts and aspects of Production System.

All of these and many more tools have delivered excellent results to organizations across the industries. For sure, during the course of its lifecycle, an organization would require most of these tools and techniques to be implanted. However, for an organization that begins its journey of Manufacturing Excellence, such a mind boggling number of tools and techniques available across disciplines, becomes overwhelming.

Actually, an organization must know, which tool or technique be applied for what purpose and when. It also means that an organization requires a simple methodology that allows it to naturally identify suitable tools or techniques necessary for carrying out improvements it is ready to take on.

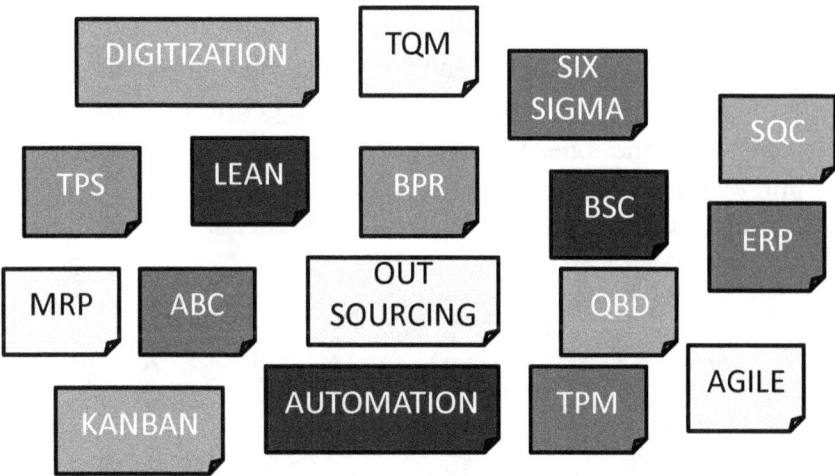

Figure 2.8 A collage of tools and techniques for improvement. Where does an organization start improvement? Which tool does it pick first? Confusion galore when an organization wants to take first step towards Manufacturing Excellence.

Apparent Complexity in Improving Production System

Just abundance of improvement techniques is not the only reason to confuse managers and engineers which one they should choose to implement. There is a next level of complexity within the organization that confuses them in where to begin improvement with.

As it happens often, it is normal for executives to know and be impressed by one of the several improvement techniques and start an implementation initiative in the organization. For example, improving performance of a Production System may mean crashing setup time (using LEAN), reducing stop time (using TPM) and stabilizing process time (using Six Sigma).

Let's consider a Production System, where the manufacturing has over 500 resources and over 2500 employees. And consider what we are used to think 'A system is sum of parts, and hence, improving all parts improves the complete system'.

Now, when we pick one technique, we tend to deploy the new found technique across 500 resources by thinking that the complete system will improve. Doing so, in fact, becomes overwhelming in terms of effort, time and resources to bring the change. We start implementing from one end of the organization to the other end (the mega roll out plan!), only to soon find ourselves into a daunting exercise. And well before we even get the sight of results, changes in business needs force us to pick another new technique of improvement.

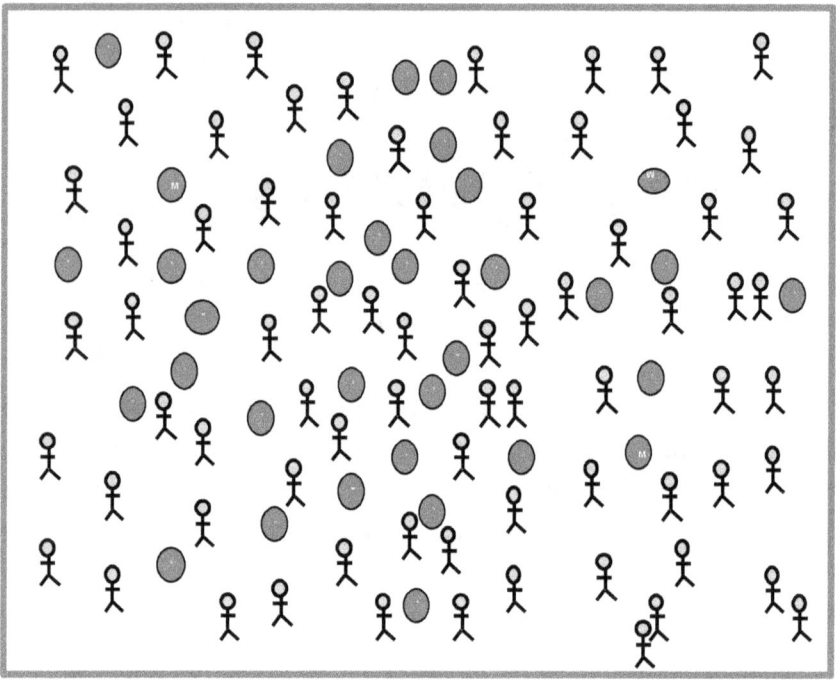

Figure 2.9 Every new initiative to improve performance faces the challenge of taking it through a mind numbing size of touch points.

Not for nothing that over 70% of initiatives promising all round transformation despite using well proven tools and techniques (and often engaging experienced consultants) either fail to deliver results or are stopped midway. And, quite a number of organizations fall into a cultural backlash that resists any further new improvement initiative.

One of the best ways to understand the psychology of apparent complexity behind improvement initiatives is to ask managers, which of the following two systems in Figure 2.10, is more complex to improve.

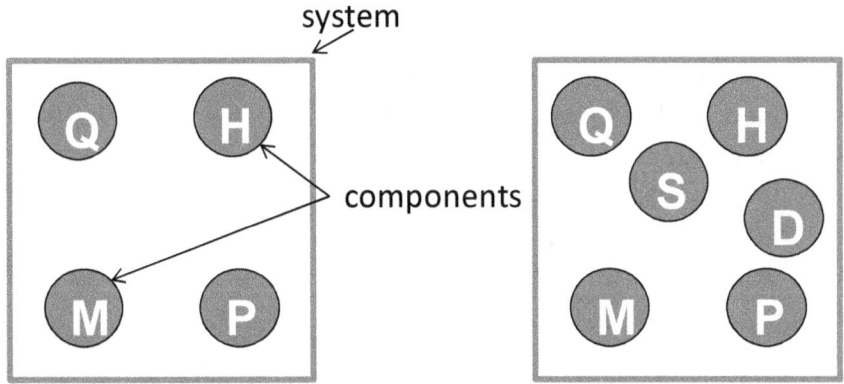

Figure 2.10 Traditional way of looking at an organization, as "Sum of parts". Which system is more difficult to improve? Obviously the second one, it has 50% more components.

The usual answer is, "Obviously, the second one. It contains 50% more components and therefore, it will require more resources, more people, more time, more effort, more money and more attention. To improve it, there will be more improvement projects." And there is truth in what people say - the detailed complexity overwhelms any thought of improvement. When the complexity overwhelms, people start trying to improve different parts of the organization in different directions, in a localized manner by whatever tools and techniques they get hold of.

Given this perspective, it is normal in organizations to find that cost improvement initiatives started in one part of the organization adversely affect quality and throughput of the entire organization. Similarly, trying to control employee cost has adverse impact on their morale and has a negative impact on the throughput of the complete organization. And, trying to improve the throughput of a shop-floor in isolation to meet production targets, often leads to production of items that lie months unsold and written off subsequently, while customer satisfaction levels for the most needed items nose dives. During each one of such presumed improvement initiatives, individual functions or departments do achieve their improvement targets, but the organization as a whole does not necessarily capture the benefit.

Managers land into such a situation because an organization is seen as 'the sum of parts' without giving clear weightage to the interfaces between the parts. They try to deal with each part separately without taking care of their impact on the rest of the system, Figure 2.11.

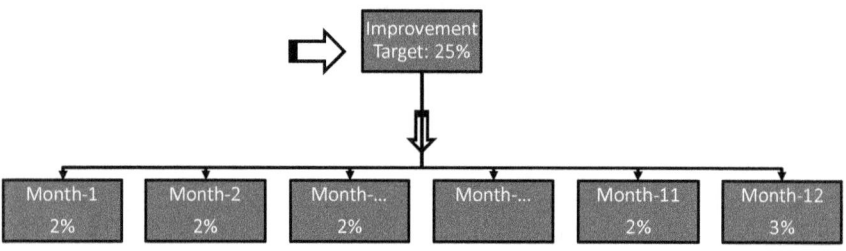

Figure 2.11 The Thinking of Organization as 'the sum of parts' is ingrained in us.

One of the key issues Managers realize during implementation of improvement programs is that Production is a system comprising a number of interrelated subsystems. They also know that each subsystem has its own goal and target (often conflicting). As a consequence, improvement in one area adversely affects improvement goals of other areas, which creates significant conflicts, chaos and resistance to change. And despite making an all out attempt to deploy even simple tools to improve all areas, the system (organization) as a whole does not make significant headway.

While Managers realize that 'the system is more than sum of parts', often they do not know what it means. They jump from one improvement to another improvement without knowing how to make an improvement that with certainty also improves performance of the organization, not just once but on an ongoing basis.

Inherent Simplicity and TOC

Every system is built with an objective and it must achieve its objective through its interdependent building blocks. Since the building blocks of a system are interdependent they not only influence the system performance, they also influence each other. As a matter of fact, *at a given time*, the improvement in performance of the system comprising a number of interconnected subsystems is dictated not by each and every subsystem, rather one or just a few, as shown by the bottom most block in Figure 2.12. This is a classical system's thinking [1].

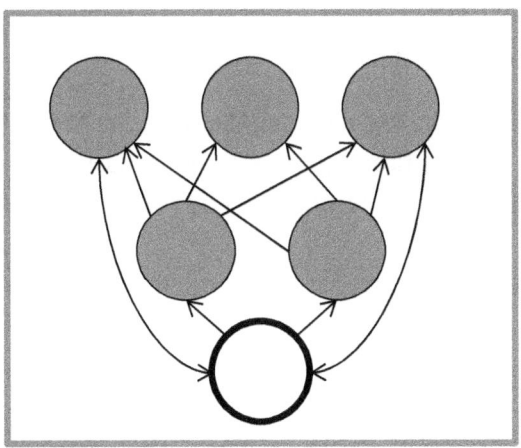

Figure 2.12 At a given time, performance of a system is dictated by one or just a few parts

Further, fundamentals of System Dynamics say, "When the interconnections are too many, the degree of freedom becomes dramatically low." Stated simply, "the reality is that however complex a system is, it is inherently simple." This simplicity exists naturally, due to dependencies of different building blocks on each other.

What it means in real life situations is that performance of a system can be improved at a given time, by influencing performance of just a few blocks and it is futile to improve all the building blocks of the system.

Production is such a system. Whether there are 10 functions, 50 departments or 500 resources, different blocks of the system are interrelated and connected by cause and effect logic. Hence, at any time, there would be just a few things that would be good enough to improve in order to improve performance of the Production System as a whole.

It also means that Managers, by their role, must be able to see these interactions between the blocks (working of the system); and in order to improve performance of the whole system quickly, must avoid dealing with all the blocks at once or individually in isolation (i.e. creating local optima). Once they see the interactions between different blocks, it becomes easy for them to establish the cause and effect between the system goal and the building blocks, and obtain significant impact on the system with minimum effort

On the other hand, since managers are always busy, if they tend to overlook the interactions between the building blocks, even a system with just a few components becomes more complex than the one with more components but with known interactions. Thus, if the interactions between the components is known, then even a system having more components will be easier to improve than the one that has less parts with unknown interactions, as shown below.

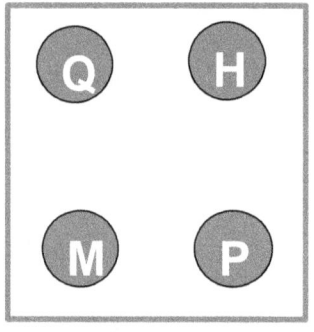   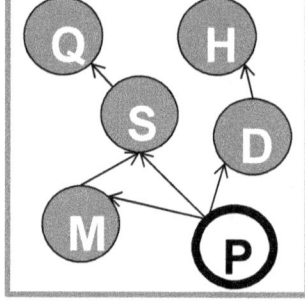

Complex to Improve   Simple to Improve

Figure 2.13 From management viewpoint, a system with known interactions between its parts is simpler than a system with unknown interaction of parts

And therefore, at any moment, Managers in Production must focus on just the few things that limit progress of their System towards its objective of improving the flow. Such a limiting element is called a Constraint. The management technique, which offers a systematic way of identifying and leveraging Constraints, is thus called Theory of Constraints. First time, it was used in solving business problems by Eli Goldratt in mid 1980s and its key concepts were popularized through his path breaking business novel 'The Goal - The Process of Ongoing Improvement' [2].

TOC- A Key to Enhanced Management Effectiveness

Recognizing that every system operates with a finite resource base, Managers must focus on just a few things that prevent the plant from reaching closer to its goal (delivering more goods within a short lead time).

In fact, the number of things, a (Plant) Manager can give attention to, is limited by the need to deliver things within short time, (the lead time being the operating horizon). Under such a situation, management attention becomes highly scarce resource. Since managers are involved in multitasking and are the key change agents, they need to pay attention to those things that are more important and urgent. Therefore, managing business by managing *Constraints* is the only way in making best of whatever time they have.

This is analogous to recognizing that an organization is like a chain comprising a number of links. And, at any time, 'strength of a chain is dictated by strength of its weakest link', Figure 2.14. Trying to strengthen any other link than the 'weakest link', does not improve strength of the chain. Hence, as a process of improvement, at a given time, it is imperative to strengthen the weakest link and not waste management attention on strengthening other links.

Figure 2.14 Strength of the Chain is limited by the strength of the Weakest Link

TOC's Five Focusing Steps

TOC equips managers with a methodology in identifying the System Constraint (weakest link) and in developing an improvement process to make "more on less", quickly. Called as Focusing Mechanism, the methodology is captured in five focusing steps, also called as 5F steps, which are [2,3]:

> Step 1. Identify the System's Constraint.
> Step 2. Decide how to Exploit the System's Constraint.
> Step 3. Subordinate everything else to the above Decision.
> Step 4. Elevate the System's Constraint.
> Step 5. If a Constraint is broken, go back to Step 1. But don't allow inertia to become a Constraint.

Applying 5 Focusing Steps to Manufacturing

As we see above, performance improvement by the five focusing steps is a cyclic process. That is why TOC is a powerful transformational methodology for ongoing improvement, Figure 2.15.

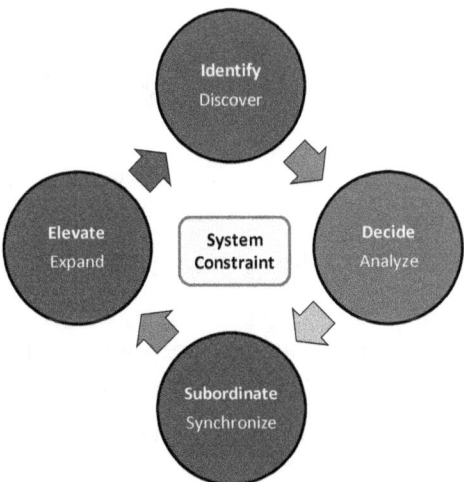

Figure 2.15 Five focusing steps provide a cyclic process of constraint management

Step-1: Identify the System Constraint (The Weakest Link)

In Production, we are used to the term Bottleneck. However, TOC uses the word capacity 'Constrained' resource, which is not same as Bottleneck.

A vast majority of studies reveal that capacity of a plant is the capacity of its people to see hidden capacity and not just the apparent capacity of its resources. In fact, the way a resource is managed, often makes it a Constraint, even if its design capacity could be higher than several other resources. This is a fundamental understanding and pivot to the thinking of Constraint Management and the belief to leverage potential of the Constraint.

According to TOC, a constrained resource faces a demand more than its apparent capacity. In a stable system that consists of a number of resources, one of the ways to identify the constrained resource is by looking at the work in progress (WIP) in the shop floor. The resource that has the longest queue of WIP would be the constraint. Alternatively, the slowest resource in a line could be constraining the line. For a linear flow line shown in the Figure 2.16a, resource C is the constrained resource. This resource dictates the throughput of the line, which as shown is 5 pieces per day.

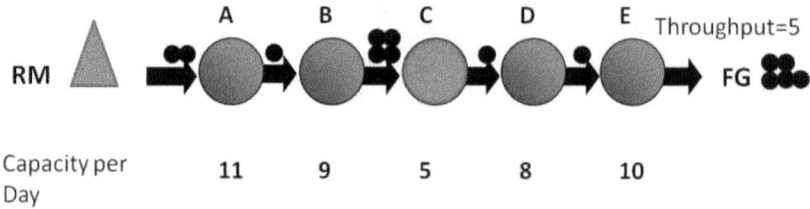

Figure 2.16a: Throughput of the line is limited by the constrained resource (5 per day)

Managers might also feel that they are traditionally used to follow Step-1. It is not just identification of the Constraint, but the real challenge is how the constraint is managed to provide a leverage point to the organization.

TOC proposes that once the Constraint is identified, the complete Plant (or line) must focus on the Constraint; since any improvement in the performance of the Constraint gives immediate benefits to the complete organization, and takes the organization immediately closer to its goal. Conversely, at a moment of time, other things remaining the same, trying to improve any other part of the Plant than the Constraint, will not improve its performance but will only lead into exhausting scarce resource of the organization, starting with management attention.

Step-2: Decide How to Exploit the System Constraint (Decision Making)

The Step-2 of the focusing mechanism, therefore, is to decide on securing the time of the Constraint such that its capacity is not wasted. An important element in securing the time of the Constraint is by creating a buffer stock of work in front of the Constraint, Figure 2.16b. The intention of using a buffer stock is meant to isolate the Constraint from disturbances that might take place upstream.

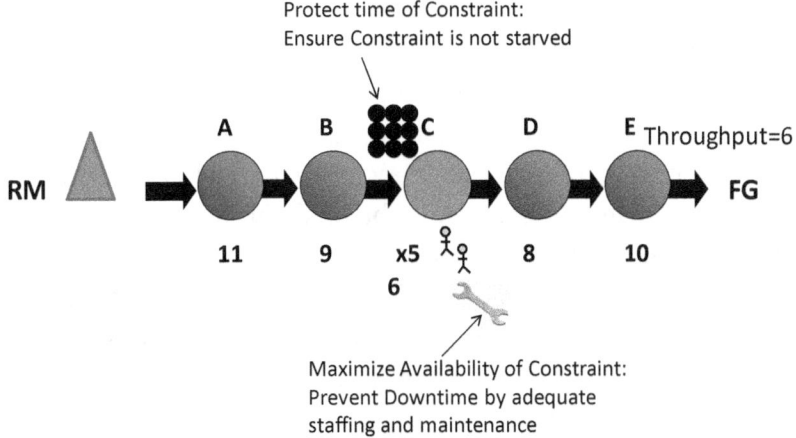

Figure 2.16b The Plant must take a decision to protect the time of the constrained resource by providing adequate work to it and ensuring that its capacity is not wasted.

In the plant, it means taking decisions to always ensure availability of just enough stock (work), in front of the constrained resource. This also means monitoring the Constraint closely and figuring out its stoppages and runtime. Now if there are stoppages like changeover, lunch break, cleaning, inspection etc, all these must be re-engineered to reduce unproductive time of the Constraint. And if any of the essential steps within or outside the Constraint's process has high variability, it must be made more stable. Any opportunity of waste reduction (through Lean) or variability reduction (through Six Sigma) that protects the time of the Constraint must be identified.

This approach of decision making called 'Decide to Exploit' the constraint is a profound way of preparing focused improvement activities on the most vital part (weakest link) of the system, thus turning weakness into strength. While taking decisions to exploit the Constraint, it is usual to identify capacity improvement opportunity in the range of 15-20%. Remembering that the Constraint limits the throughput of the line, therefore, an improvement of 15% utilization of the Constraint means an improvement of 15% for the entire line. *Yes, an hour gained of the Constraint is an hour gained for the entire line [2].*

Compare this with the traditional approach of measuring utilization of all resources, and trying to keep them always busy to achieve high utilization or justify return on asset. In the traditional way of working, when the plant management runs after so many resources, its attention is diluted everywhere, and effectiveness of the precious management time is blunted. In fact, many times its attention misses the constraint. For the same reason, piles of inventory are kept in front of *all resources* to prevent them from starvation. This keeps all resources very busy and make shop floor look like a battlefield. Of course, it leads to a huge work in progress (WIP), hides defects, elongates lead time, increases cost, creates chaos and generates conflicts. No wonder, insufficient attention is paid on the real constrained resource. And then, suddenly nobody loves production, people find their work and home life unbalanced and they start complaining that there is a capacity problem.

The Step-2 allows the Production Team to initiate the process of increasing focus on the Constraint and take decision of exploiting (leverage) its time, so that its hidden capacity is revealed immediately. And it is seen that often, a mere decision making exercise with the team working on the constrained resource, dramatically improves attention on improving its performance. As a result, performance of the constrained resource improves (to 6 units per day in the example shown in Figure 2.16b). However, Step 2 is not sufficient in itself and the decisions taken to exploit the Constraint must be implemented to harness the real power of focusing methodology.

Step-3: Subordinate to the Decision to Exploit the System Constraint (Synchronized Action)

In this step, everybody across the flow of the process orders subordinates to the decisions taken to exploit the Constraint, since it dictates the rate of movement of the organization towards its goal.

This is the step that aligns all the parts of Production and external system to the rhythm of the Constraint. TOC asks the over capacity, better performing and more capable resources, functions, department and subsystem to subordinate to the rhythm of the Constraint. *This calls for a dramatic change in behavior across the flow; and bringing in such a change (of behavior) is not trivial.* During the process of alignment, when an organization focuses on the Constraint, it helps people who work around the Constraint to identify the extra hidden capacity.

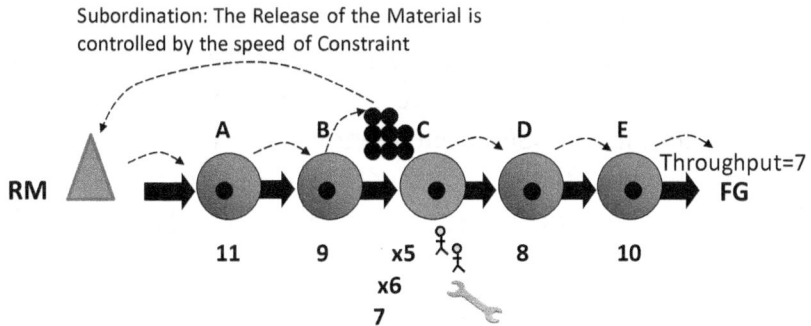

Figure 2.16c The Release of the material is done at the rhythm of the Constraint

'Subordination' is a dirty word in today's society. But in a team and a system, subordination to the overall Goal and therefore, to exploitation of the cause that limits progress towards the Goal, is an essence of team spirit. In the context of Production, it means that non constrained resources and functions must ensure that serving the Constraint is on the top of their action plan and their local strategies are geared to maximizing utilization of the Constraint. It means that

1. The resources upstream to the Constraint consciously avoid becoming haughty of their overcapacity and eschew student syndrome (procrastination till the last minute). It is often seen that once a resource is declared as the Constraint, others thump up their chest and relax believing that they have huge time advantage over the Constraint and could catch up with its speed anytime. Hence, the resources that precede Constraints, often get into negligence and laziness, run into student syndrome and try to catch up at the last moment. However, uncertainties and Murphy are always alive and kicking, and they strike at the most unfortunate times. Any

failure of feeder resources or functions to ensure sufficient work at the Constraint, immediately results in a loss of throughput of the complete plant (or line). We already know that *an hour lost on the constraint is an hour lost for the complete plant or line.*

2. Eschewing student syndrome does not mean that the upstream resources produce as much as possible and stock huge inventory in front of the Constraint. The inventory in front of the Constraint is a protective inventory (as per step-2), which is just enough to prevent it from starving. Once the protective stock is built at the Constraint, if the upstream resources produce more than the rate of the Constraint, it will only create extra inventory and create chaos upstream. Chaos in the upstream will prevent responsiveness and natural advantage of the upstream system and would subsequently, jeopardize utilization of the Constraint. It is advisable to let the upstream idle with some extra capacity, so that there is enough slack in the system to catch up, if anything goes broke upstream.

In order to guarantee that neither the constrained resource is starved nor the floor is over flooded, the release of the material to the gating operation (resource A) is controlled by the rhythm of the constrained resource (as shown by a long arrow of communication from resource C to the Raw Material, RM in Figure 2.16c).

3. The resources downstream to the Constraint could also fall into an undesirable behavior trap. It is the responsibility of the downstream resources to be always in a ready to serve state or relay race behavior to pick and run, as soon as the Constraint delivers the work. This is because, with focus on the Constraint, if the work order processed by the Constraint is delayed by sloppiness of resource downstream, all the effort in improving utilization (exploitation) of the Constraint is wasted.

4. Take also the case of support departments like, Supply Chain, HR, Quality, Maintenance, Finance etc. All must ensure that amongst their whole lot of daily list of activities, they give priority to the needs of the Constraint, in case their attention is needed.

For example, if a breakdown takes place at the Constraint, maintenance department ensures that its team first attends to the constrained resource. Similarly, if it is found that in order to exploit the Constraint, an expense is inevitable; despite difficult times; the Finance department must subordinate to the need of the Constraint and release funds on fast track to speed up service to the Constraint, since the Constraint is a Goldmine. Similarly, quality department must ensure that the work orders passing through the constrained resource are pre-screened and flawless. The same is applicable to the HR and raw material procurement policies. Thus we see that managing by the Constraint forces all other process to have their priority synchronized and if needed, improve their own processes around the Constraint. Indirectly, when an organization manages constraints on an ongoing basis, its other aspects including quality and costs automatically improve. At this stage of Subordinating to the Decision to Exploit the Constraint, the flow of the plant or line improves dramatically, (to 7 pieces per day in the example shown in Figure 2.16c).

Step-4: Elevate the System Constraint (Expand Capacity)

Only when the Constraint is fully improved to the level, where further improvement by exploitation leads to the law of diminishing returns or the demand for products processed by the Constraint increases too much significantly, the capacity of the Constraint is elevated. Elevating the capacity of the Constraint can be obtained say, by increasing the scheduled hours, by installing new resource, by adding more manpower, by outsourcing the specific process etc, Figure 2.16d.

Elevation entails significant effort, time, money and management attention. Hence, organizations need to be cautious in taking elevation route, until all the possibilities of exploitation is exhausted. In the traditional way of management, often it is seen that Managers resort to Elevation before Exploitation, which not only prevents the organizations in adopting a stable ongoing process of improvement, it also brings in significant risks.

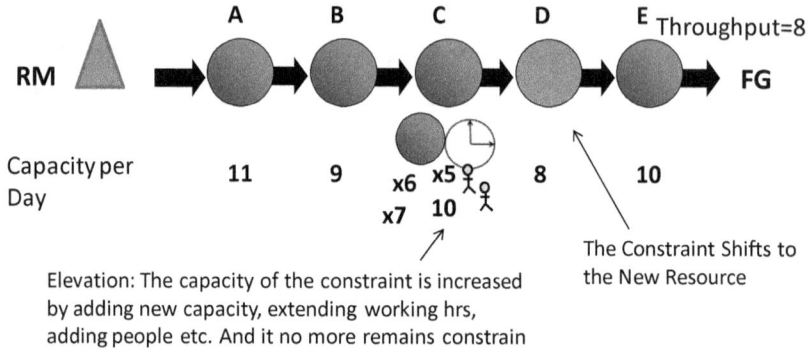

Figure 2.16d: Once the law of diminishing return plays in, the constrained resource is elevated and it no more remains the constraint.

Step-5: Repeat the Cycle

When capacity of the Constraint is elevated, the resource does not remain a Constraint any more (capacity of resource C becomes 10 pieces per day while that of D is still 8 pieces per day). If the demand happens to be more than 8 pieces, it becomes important to go back to the Step-1 of the Five Focusing Steps and take the organization to the next cycle of progressive improvement.

When the next constraint is identified, some of the rules set while exploiting the previous constraints may need to be revisited and the operations is aligned to the new constraint. Thus we see that TOC provides a progressive cyclic process of ongoing improvement.

When substantial elevation is done at the Constraint, the capacity of the line increases and a lot of spare capacity is created. Sometimes, in a single line plant, it might also mean that production no more remains a constraint, i.e. the supply from the line is more than the demand. Then, it needs to be fed by more process orders, which actually means that the Constraint has moved over to the Market.

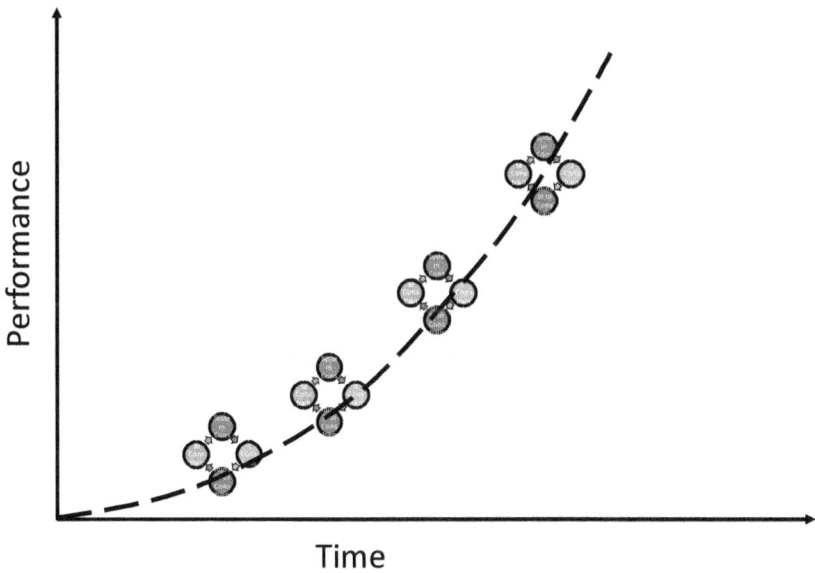

Figure 2.16e TOC is a management approach for building the process of ongoing improvement

Also, often the Constraint is not necessarily a physical resource inside the plant. The decision to exploit and the diligent process of synchronization with the constraint give significant insights into this aspect.

A Production System comprises a number of functions and departments, while Production itself is a part of a bigger organizational system, where each element influences some other and the organization as a whole. The interrelated subsystems on an ongoing basis need to subordinate to the requirements of the Constraint (weakest link), thus forcing a continuous churn in the policies laid out for operating and improving the system. As a result of following five focusing steps, the organizational policies as well as structures align to manage the organization, the TOC way. In fact, a vast majority of constraints are Policy Constraints and not Resource Constraints. A Resource Constraint will often give a signal towards other types of constraints. For example, while exploiting a constrained resource, it could be found that prevailing high rate of absenteeism of operators causes its stoppages and poor utilization. An analysis to the observation might take one to question the HR policy of the organization.

The Path to Responsive Production System

The ongoing process of making Production more responsive can be summarized in following steps.

1. Classify offerings (products) as MTA or MTO based on the promise made to the market.
2. Place a mechanism to generate process orders only based upon consumption from stock (MTA) or customer order (MTO).
3. Establish criteria to allow a single priority system for products and within products for the process orders.
4. Follow the single priority system.
5. Identify products which are chronically in shortage of deliveries. If the process of identification is cumbersome, pick those products where the organization wants to improve deliveries.
6. Trace the flow of these products backward from dispatch warehouse to raw material warehouse.
7. Quickly identify the stage that determines the flow of these products and pin down the constrained resource.
8. Communicate across the flow and supporting functions about the location of the constraint.
9. Ensure that enough buffer work is available for the constraint.
10. Tightly schedule the constraint to minimize leakage of its available time and synchronize the release of material at the gating operation to the pace of the constraint.
11. Ensure that the downstream resources are always ready to serve the constraints and move fast as soon as the constraint delivers a work.
12. Seek collaboration of the staff working on the constraint to improve its utilization.

13. Brain storm with the local teams to clearly identify the improvement actions needed on the constraint and the expected specific throughput improvement.
14. Facilitate and train the staff to implement improvement actions. Use the known techniques from Lean, Six Sigma, TQM, TPM etc to improve performance of the constraint.
15. Drive an improvement plan on the constraint with shift-wise review of constraint's operations e.g. process time, stop time, setup time, improvement actions etc.
16. On regular basis, the constraint might get disrupted; ensure that the root causes of the disruption are systematically analyzed using TQM tools and actions are taken promptly.
17. Ensure that supporting functions provide the highest level of service (priority) to the constraint. If required activate the desired SLAs.
18. Institute policies and SOPs according to the new way of managing the production line.
19. Improve the performance of the constraint to the level, where the law of diminishing returns comes into play.
20. If the resource (process) is still a constraint, find ways to expand its capacity by extending shifts, outsourcing, off loading work to other resources, adding new machine, adding more people etc.
21. If the resource no more remains the constraint, go back to identify the constraining resource and start managing the constraint again. Ensure that the attention and operating policies of the organizations are focused on the new constraint.

Figure 2.17, shows an abstracted flow chart of the above steps involved in improving Operations on an ongoing basis.

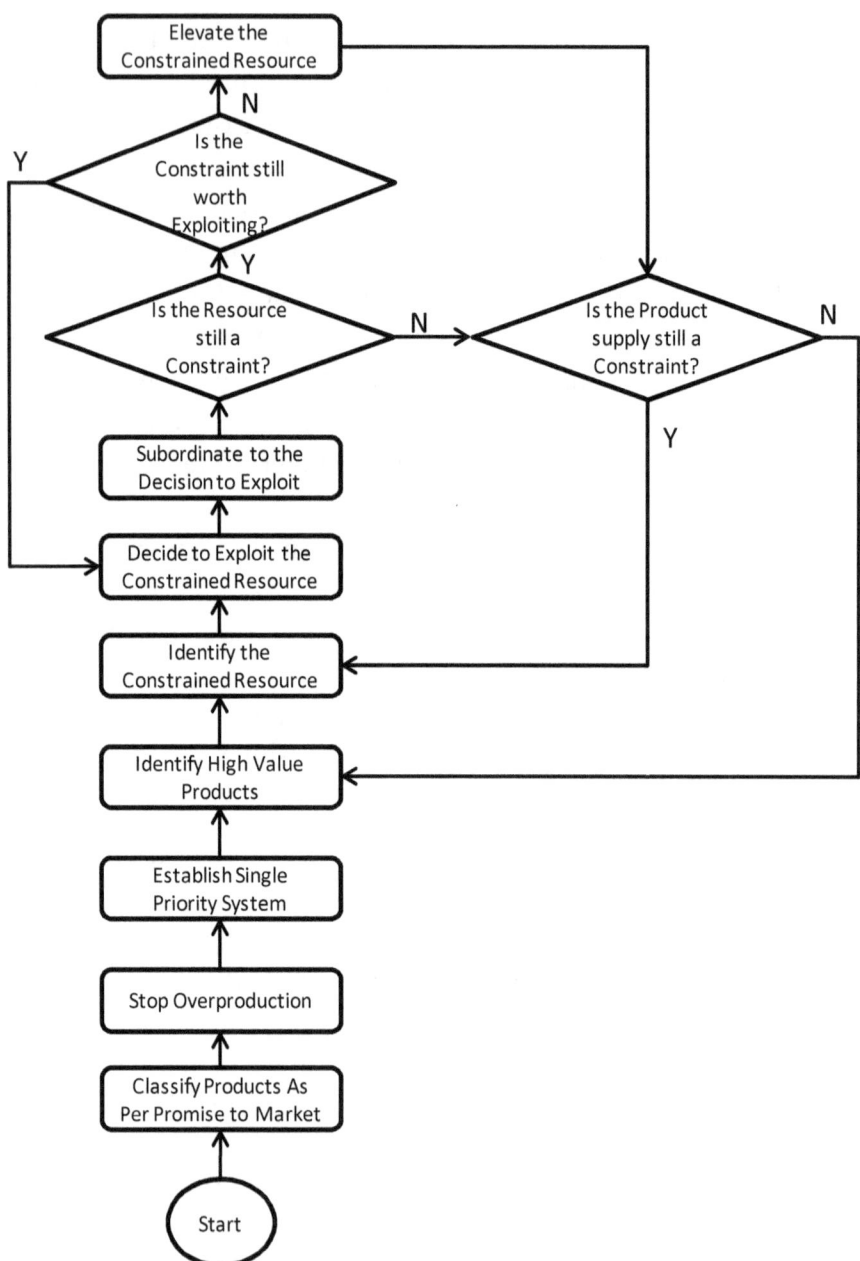

Figure 2.17: The Process of Ongoing Improvement in Operations

Improving Only Operations is not Enough for Global Competitiveness

Once focused improvement process is set in Operations, it releases substantial capacity and improves key metrics (throughput, response time, flexibility, quality and cost). This helps the organization in becoming a preferred supplier in the market. As a result, demand for its products increases and the revenue sees significant upside.

Since the improvement in performance is achieved rapidly without exhausting too many resources and without taking real risk, both the expenses and investment are relatively low. Lower expenses reinforce the already improved profitability from increased revenues. At the same time, lower investment along with faster lead time provides the organization with significant higher cash in hand. A situation like this, on an ongoing basis means that the organization is on the path of ongoing improvement (Operational Excellence) and its next need is to sustain the improvement culture in the FUTURE too.

While the organization achieves superlative operational performance and reveals free capacity, its capability and extra capacity must be capitalized. One of the ways to capitalize on the improved performance of Operations is to feed it with more customer orders by improving Sales.

However, with time, products do get obsolete, markets do get saturated, competitors emerge with new products, product prices nose dive, customers demand change, etc. The long term growth of the organization, therefore, depends on how it deals with these issues by regularly turning out new and competitive products.

A good thing for the Product Development function is that, when the Operations is being managed the TOC way, the Production is already well oiled to take extra load of new products. Thus, the Product Development function is left with the responsibility to bring out new products faster and reinforce the organization on its path of ongoing improvement. Thus, as shown in Figure 2.18, we see that the capability of Operations and that of Product Development feed into each other. This is the virtuous cycle, world class manufacturing organizations must aim to build.

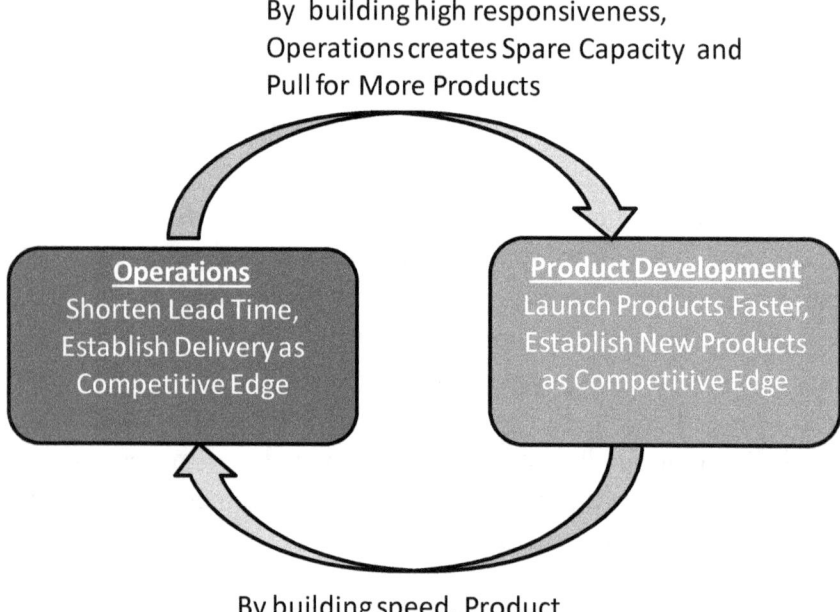

Figure 2.18 Operations and Product Development Feed into Each other.

Rapid Product Development

The Complexity of Product Development

Development of a new product takes much longer duration than the lead time of Operations. Sometimes it is months and sometimes years. Product Development is, therefore, conducted in the format of a project, where a set of activities are conducted to deliver a set of product features within a limited time and resource.

In an ever changing environment, even though the process of product development has a longer time horizon than that of operations, an organization must develop its new products at an ever faster pace.

Studies carried out in the domain of project management reveal that a vast majority of projects fail to deliver their intended objectives of time, scope and cost, primarily because of the uncertainties. A large part of uncertainty enter the project environment just because projects are long duration affairs (long duration invites uncertainties) and projects are human intensive (behavior and emotions play their part in creating uncertainties).

The secret of completing projects on time seems to be dependent on the ability of the team to deal with uncertainties. Since the investors actually see their returns only upon commissioning the project, the Due Date Performance (DDP) of the project becomes a key performance metric for the Product Development function.

The Process of Project Management

A project passes through following broad phases:

1. Scoping: A project is broken down into work packages that are delivered by executing a number of tasks.

2. Sequencing: Tasks are sequenced in series or parallel based on their inter dependencies and logistics of the process of development.

3. Estimation: The implementation team provides estimated duration of each task. The longest sequence of tasks called

the critical path is recorded. The critical path dictates the duration of the project.

4. Scheduling: The complete project is time-lined in detail at task as well as activity level; and then intermediate milestones are *agreed and committed.*

5. Resource Allocation: Resources are assigned to each task.

6. Costing: Estimation of people time, materials and service components for each task and phase wise costing for the project is *agreed and committed.*

7. Execution: The project is monitored, reviewed and controlled to deliver the agreed features as per schedule and cost.

The blueprint and details of above steps are captured in a Project Plan Document.

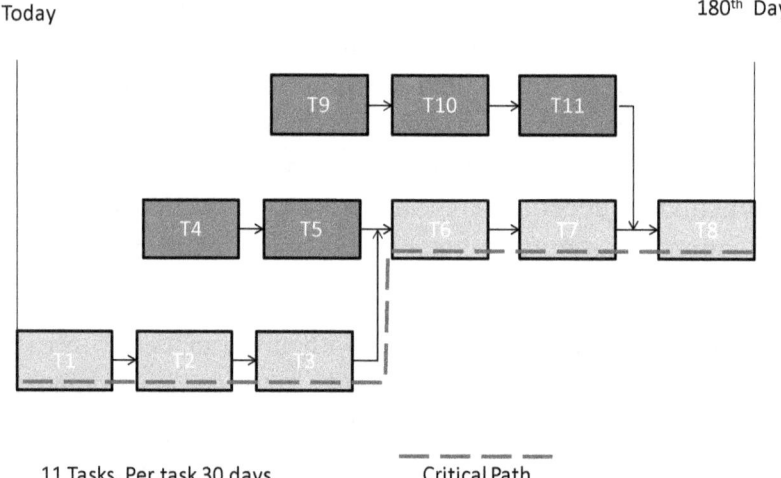

11 Tasks, Per task 30 days   Critical Path

Figure 3.1 The Critical Path dictates the duration of the project

As projects become larger and as organizations handle multiple (sub) projects, the above steps may go through several iterations of corrections. There are several tools and training programs to help in managing projects better.

From the above, Project Management looks simple and straight forward, but in reality why do over 70% of projects fail to meet their objective?

Following reasons are often mentioned to highlight delays in projects, irrespective of their type and length:

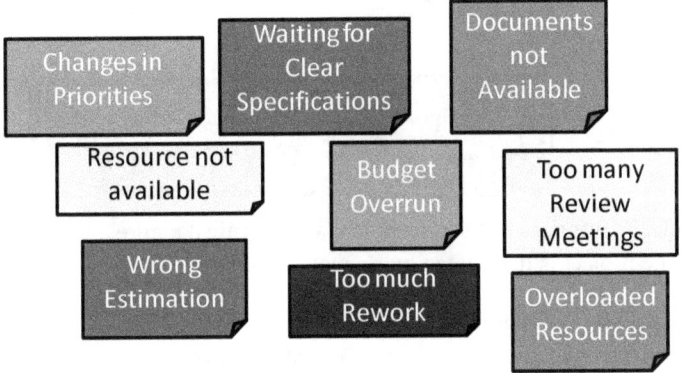

Figure 3.2 The most common highlighted reasons of delays in Projects

Apparent Complexity of Project Environment

In a project based organization, people are technically competent in their tasks and organizations do recruit and assign competent people in projects. A project consists of two broad aspects:

1. Technical aspect (the knowledge of technology involved in product development and what to do technically) and

2. Management aspect (the process of project management including logistics of activities).

Normally, organizations are built around reasonably sound technical competencies and then, other management competencies are appended with time.

In fact, a vast majority of organizations has significant certainty in its technical competencies. But, since organizations traditionally build themselves with technical competencies, they tend to neglect managerial competencies. This lopsided approach (for good reason) leads to significant delays in the overall lead time of product development.

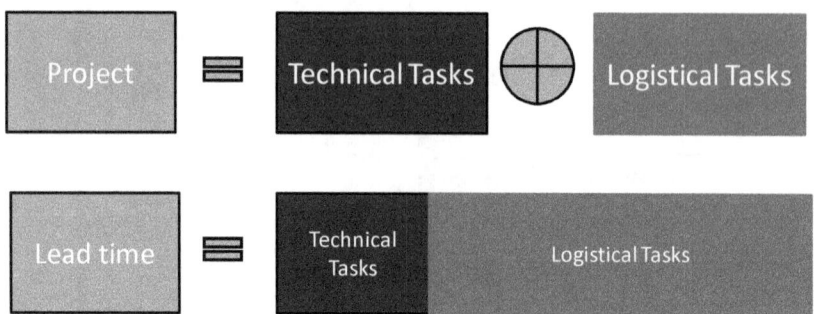

Figure 3.3 A project comprises tasks of technical and logistical nature, but often the lead time of the project is dominated by Logistical Tasks

Furthermore, since traditionally there has been less focus on managerial issues of product development, projects are marred with a high level of uncertainty that often account for more than 30% and in several cases over 70% of the product development lead time.

Nevertheless, a Product Development function owns responsibility of time to market and is measured by precise metrics of DDP, number of new products per year, cycle time and people productivity. And, the function, functional heads, managers and developers are measured on what they commit on these metrics. Thus, although *projects by nature belong to a probabilistic environment, organizations tend to measure people in a deterministic way.* Expectedly, this creates significant conflicts within the organization. No doubt so many projects go haywire and they see delays of as much as 300% of estimated time. Let's look deeper into some of the areas where despite availability of best resources and practices, projects get delayed perennially.

Estimation:

Estimations are estimations; and as we know they are never accurate. Any given task has a level of variability and it is never possible to give an accurate estimate (commitment). In fact, a task estimate can only be given by a degree of confidence or probability of completion.

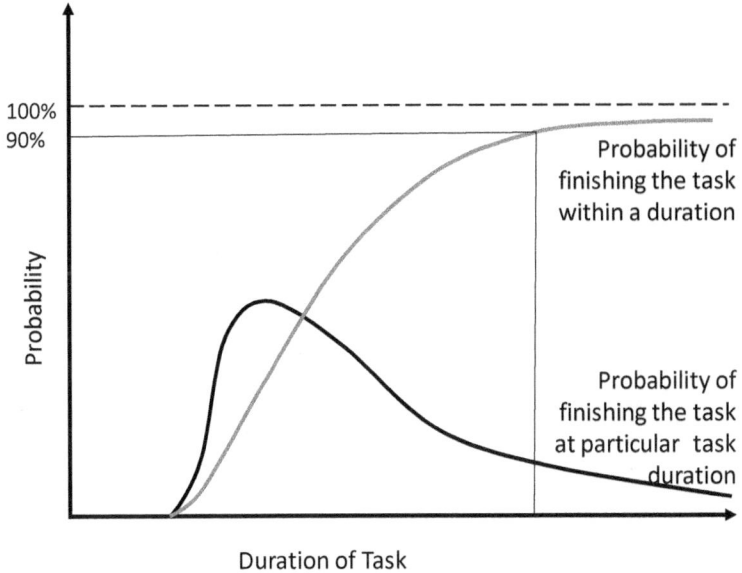

Figure 3.4 There is no accurate duration of a Task, it has a probabilistic nature

However, in most organizations, people providing estimations are measured on their estimation. Their estimations are considered as commitments and tied to their performance appraisals and annual increments. With time, people become wiser and start giving pessimistic estimate that could often be at 90% probability of completion. Which means a task duration estimates at more than 2 times of that at 50% probability of completion.

Hence, at the estimation stage, schedule of the project elongates. It means that higher budget and poor ROI creep into the project at planning level.

But if people add safety at each task, then projects must have better Due Date Performance. However, the truth is that despite this, projects have awfully poor DDP performance.

Execution:

As mentioned, estimations are estimations, and they may be at 70% or 90% degree of confidence. It means that there is still a 10 to 30% probability of delays over and above the estimation.

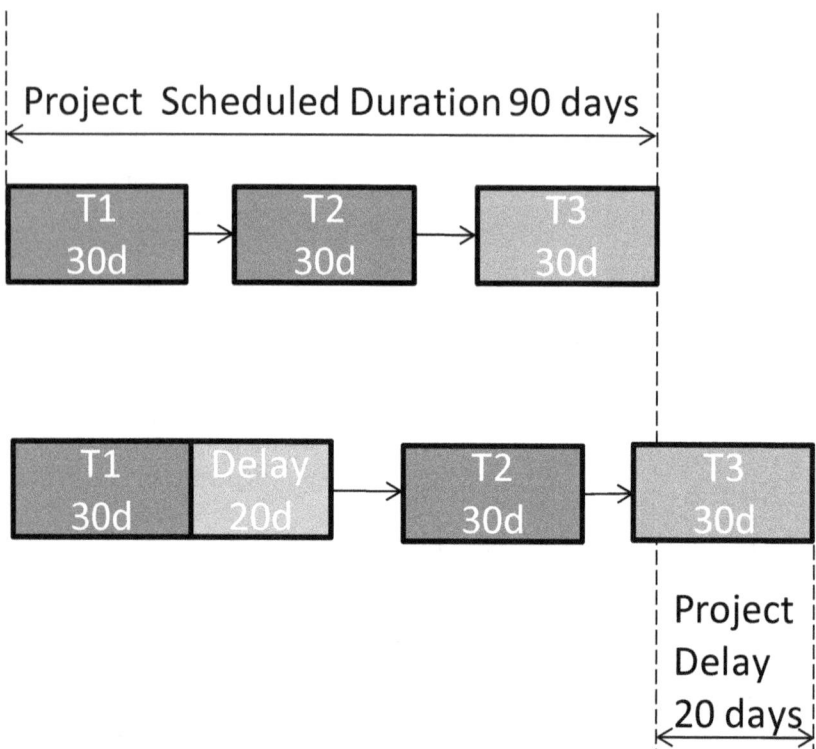

Figure: 3.5 A delay in a task delays the entire Project

And since, Project Managers know that development resources often give estimation of tasks pessimistically; they sequence the tasks tightly with strict milestones and deadlines. This happens despite the best practices of Project Management exhorting Managers to keep sufficient slack between tasks. As a result of tight scheduling, a delay in one task along the critical path leads to delay of the complete project, Figure 3.5.

At the same time if any task finishes early, it does not necessarily means that the next task will start early, because the next resource may not be free or necessary preparation is still awaited (a consequence of tight scheduling), Figure 3.6

Also there are instances especially at integration stages, where even if several of parallel tasks are finished on time or earlier, the next task can't start in time, since the entire feeder tasks must be completed, Figure 3.7.

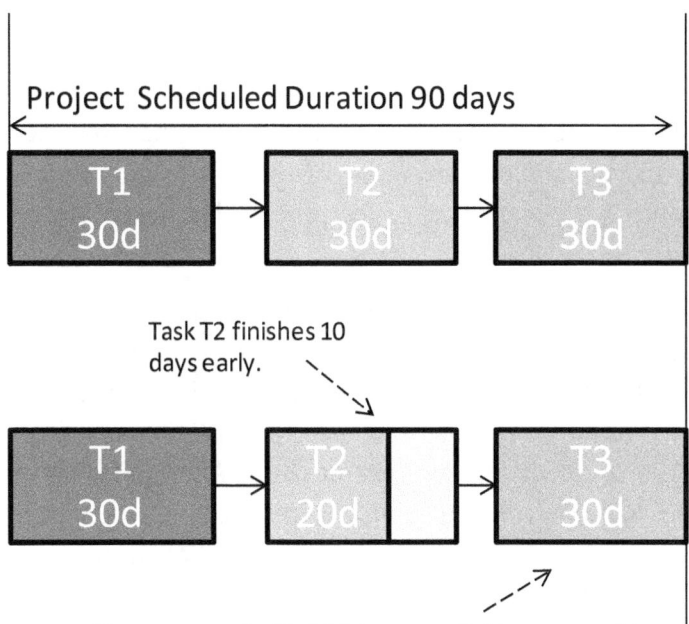

Figure 3.6: Completion of a task early does not mean early completion of project, since the tasks are often scheduled too tight

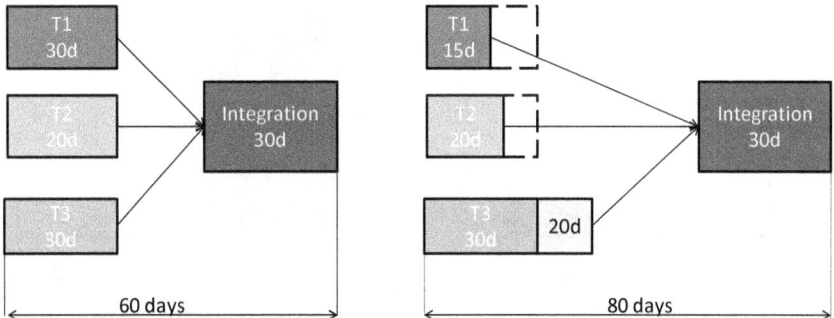

Figure 3.7 A delay in any task feeding into integration point even if other tasks are finished in time causes the Project to be late.

Thus, the way a project is estimated and its tasks are negotiated, it can only get hurt by delay in tasks but can't make over the lost time if some tasks finish in time.

Behavior Drives Results

The above is a logical explanation, but organizations consist of people who are the key stakeholders in the projects. And, people's emotions and perceptions are stronger than logic. Something else happens during the execution of the project that delays the project dramatically.

As a project moves into execution phase, since there is significantly higher buffer in each task, there is a tendency for development resources to fall into 'Student Syndrome'. In fact, *people relax at the start time of the task, expecting to catch up with most of the work near the end time of the task.* It is often seen that despite the best of technical abilities, people force themselves to exert extra effort under tremendous tension and resort to escalation and expediting at the last moment.

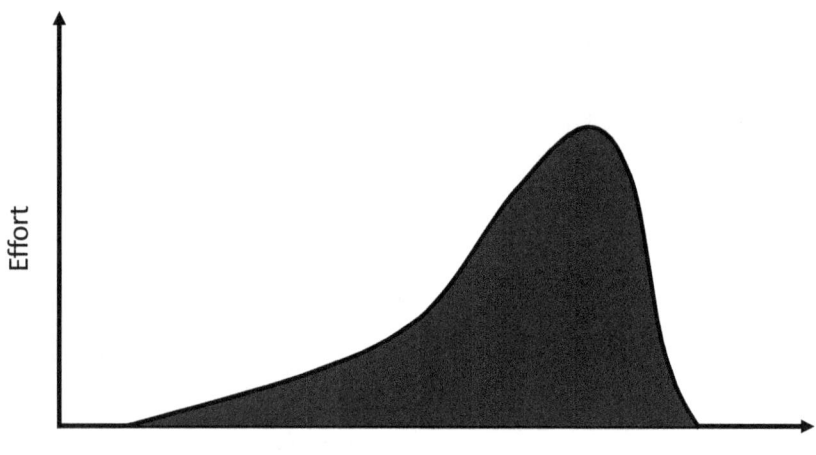

Duration Allocated for the Task

Figure 3.8 Student syndrome is a fundamental cause of loss in time during execution of the project

Actually, when you sleep down for a long time, nothing happens in the project. But, only when you start working on the task, you come to face uncertainties. Also, tasks delivered under the pressure that is accumulated by student syndrome, often leads to suboptimal delivery in scope and quality. The certainty of tasks getting late due to student syndrome is accentuated by the fact that Murphy and uncertain events do occur and often, at unexpected times. Murphy is the traditional representation of saying, "Anything that can go wrong will go wrong" or "Some or other thing will always go wrong".

This leads to delay in tasks, even when huge buffer is built within them. Further, if one task gets late, all the downstream tasks get late, making the entire project late and miss the prime objective of On Time Delivery.

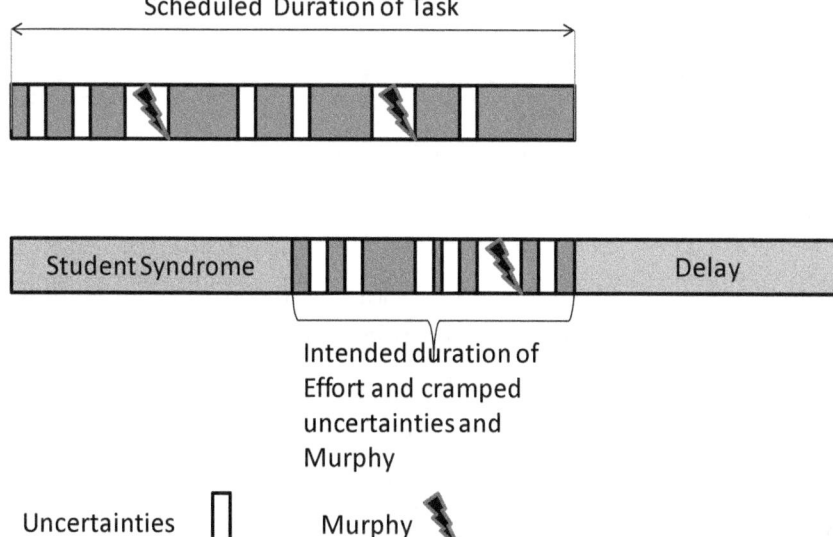

Figure 3.9: Student syndrome with uncertainty and Murphy are disastrous for Projects

Well! Let's accept, when somebody says that the task owner is not lazy. However, the other part of the world is besotted with Parkinson's Law that comes into play during the entire duration of a task. It says that *work expands with time*. That is, even when a work can be done in a much shorter time, people will always find enough work to fill the time and it would appear that the time taken by the task owner is actually the estimated duration of the task. Figure 3.10 illustrates how Parkinson's Law creeps into the project time.

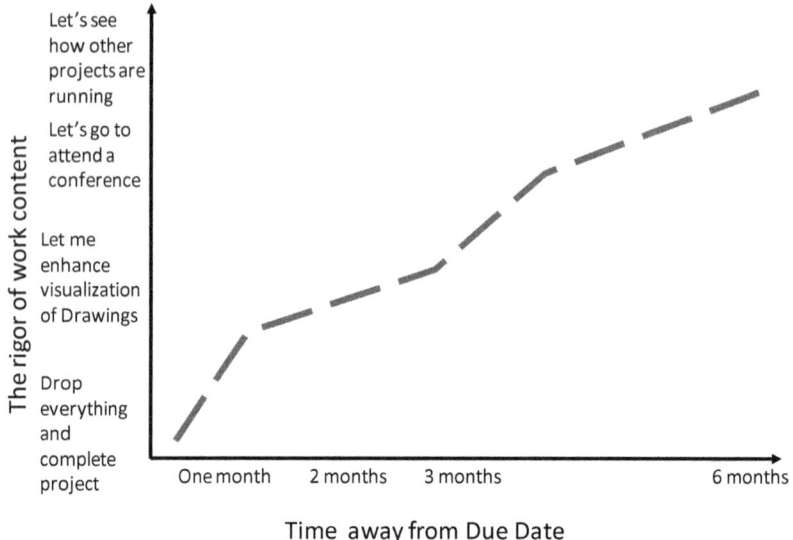

Figure 3.10 Parkinson's Law along with the way expectations are set on people's performance prevents early completion of a task.

We can say that all these are behavioral issues, but when we have more of such issues, why do not Project Managers know if the task could have been completed earlier?

Since people are measured, rewarded and reprimanded for their estimation and commitment, even when they complete their tasks in time, they do not report the right time of completion of the task. This is because completion of the tasks early may let the Project Managers recalibrate their estimates in the next task or project, and that leads the development resources into a vicious cycle of arguments, which they do not want to get into.

Now, you know the devastating impact of Student Syndrome and Parkinson's Law have on the performance of a project, when people are measured in a deterministic way, while the environment offered to them is a probabilistic one.

Actually, for an estimation based on a confidence level of 70% to 90%, more than 70% of the tasks would finish well within time. But neither the Project Manager nor the Project itself ever gets the benefit. All these because people behave the way you measure them. So, it is not a surprise that over 70% of projects fail to deliver their promised outcome.

Now, since the duration of each task of a project is cast into stone by arguing, convincing and negotiating (and sometime intimidating) with the task owner, it falls on the shoulders of the Project Manager (PM) to see that the tasks are delivered as per agreement. In fact, the PM would have also communicated the Project Plan to the superiors and the customer.

The role of a Project Manager then over-occupies with monitoring each and every task, and reviewing progress of the project with the implementation members.

Since each task has its own estimation, and estimations are never accurate even when they are on pessimistic side, a number of tasks keep on falling behind schedule. On an ongoing basis, a Project Manager keeps fire fighting, while trying to facilitate progress of one task after another. It is often found that Project Managers build a long list of 'TO DO' things and keep shuttling from one review meeting to another, reducing their effectiveness and efficiency, and thus jeopardizing progress of the project.

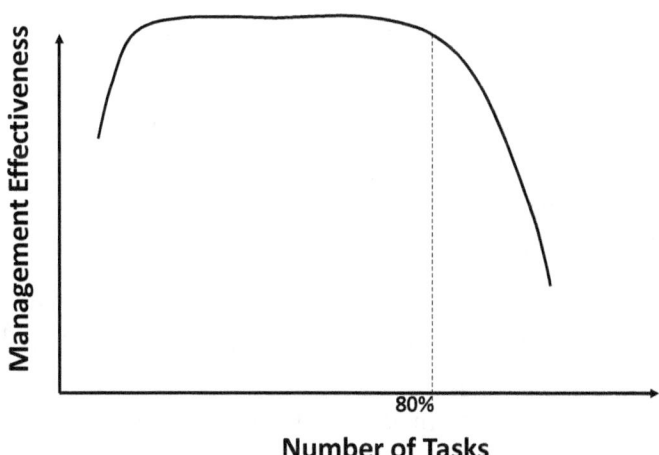

Figure 3.11: Effectiveness of a Project Manager dilutes dramatically as more tasks pileup for attention

In large projects and in a multi-project environment, the Project Manager is just like an angry bull in a ring. Since the Project Manager is the prime owner of a project, is also the key decision maker whose time is the most critical for the progress of the project. A Project Manager should spend time on most critical things, however, the current way of monitoring leaves very little scope of improvement in the way ones time is wasted. Figure 3.11 shows how effectiveness of Project Managers falls dramatically when the number of items on their TO DO list increases.

So we find that Project Managers carry too many tasks and overload themselves, which divide their attention too thin; and they are not able to pay attention to crucial issues, while projects get ever delayed.

Bad multitasking - The Dominant reason for Delays

Often, a resource is allocated to multiple tasks in one project or multiple projects, which is natural. However, as the project goes into execution phase, task after task gets late for various valid reasons. And since there are different owners for different projects and modules, the teams often land into dynamic resource contention.

Under such a situation, the Module or Project owner who has the loudest voice or connections gets the allocation of resource. And then, quite often there are dictates from the top to speed-up some or other project or task. And then, there are personal preferences. These lead to pulling of resources midcourse from one task or one project to another.

While multitasking is important at individual levels, in a complex interrelated project environment, switching between tasks leads to bad multitasking. In day to day work, Bad Multitasking often goes unnoticed but it leads to major delays in the projects. It is estimate that Bad Multitasking causes a minimum of 30% of delays in the projects, and it hurts the ROI of both the project team as well as the sponsoring agency.

Figure 3.12 illustrates the catastrophic effect of bad multitasking. We see here three tasks each of 15 days assigned probably to a team. If the team does the tasks sequentially, it would finish the projects on 15th, 30th and 45th day. But due to switching midway between tasks, the team could finish the first project only on 35th day, a time overrun of over 100%. Consider the tasks to be large enough projects of 15 months each and then try to see the impact it would have on the Due Date Performance and Return On Investment. Disastrous, isn't it!

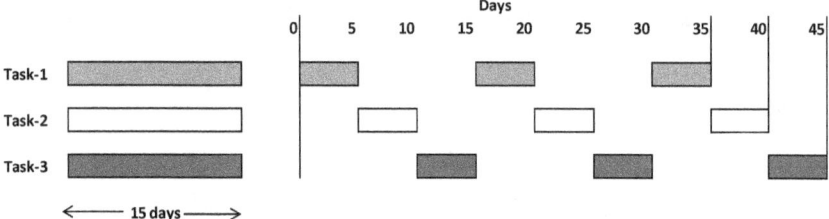

Figure 3.12: Bad Multitasking is perhaps the single most dominant reason of delays due to tentativeness of management decisions

Thus, we see that despite the best tools of project management used by an organization, projects get delayed because project environment is a network of tasks, where estimation, execution, monitoring and control have a lot of uncertainty. In order to take care of these uncertainties, we need to get into the root cause of these delays.

1. Estimation and Planning: Pessimism at task level estimation, considering estimates as commitment and overlooking resource contentions

2. Execution: Student syndrome, Parkinson's law, Murphy, bad multitasking, tight reviewing of all tasks

Improving Product Development - the TOC Way

TOC solution to improve performance of projects is based on fundamentally logistical as well as behavioral issues. These often seem common sense based and are well recognized. However, what's lacking today is the way to use these commonsense insights and build a systematic approach that prevents the gross delays, while letting organizations execute their projects in a sustainable way.

1. Estimation and Planning:

The traditional practice of including safety at each task ignores a very fundamental principle of aggregation. Along the critical path (the longest sequence of dependent tasks), probabilities multiply with the tasks and dramatically reduce the chance of completing projects on time. Here is an example in Figure 3.13. Here, each task is represented by two boxes; the second box represents uncertain part of the task.

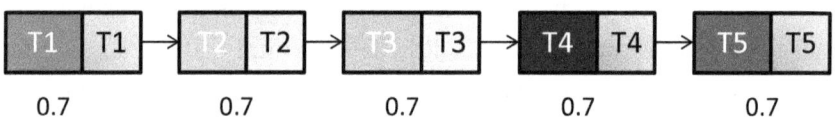

```
Each Task Duration on Critical Path, days = 30
Project Scheduled days = 150
Probability of completing each task = 0.7 (70%)
Then, Probability of finishing the project within 150days
= 0.7x0.7x0.7x0.7x0.7= 0.17 ~ 17%
```

Figure 3.13 Effect of variability and dependency on the due date performance leads to very low probability of project completing in time

There are five tasks each with a 70% probability of completing in time. What is the probability that the project will be completed before time?

A possible logic tells us that it is 17%, much less than what our intuition would indicate!

Fundamentals of statistics say that, this situation demands use of the Law of Aggregation. There is a mathematical treatment, which says that if the variability of each element of a group is aggregated then the overall variability reduces dramatically. We do see application of this principle in Insurance business, where risk of millions of people is aggregated at the Insurance company level to obtain overall low risk and thereby offering an affordable premium to individuals. And so is in the aggregation of stocks in supply chain, where stocks are located and designed by taking the benefit of aggregation at the upstream nodes.

Using this logic, TOC advices the safety be taken out of each task and be provided at the end of the Critical Path, Figure 3.14.

The idea is that we need to protect the project even if some tasks get late. This uses the benefit of aggregation of several interacting tasks that have high uncertainty. We need to understand it a little better.

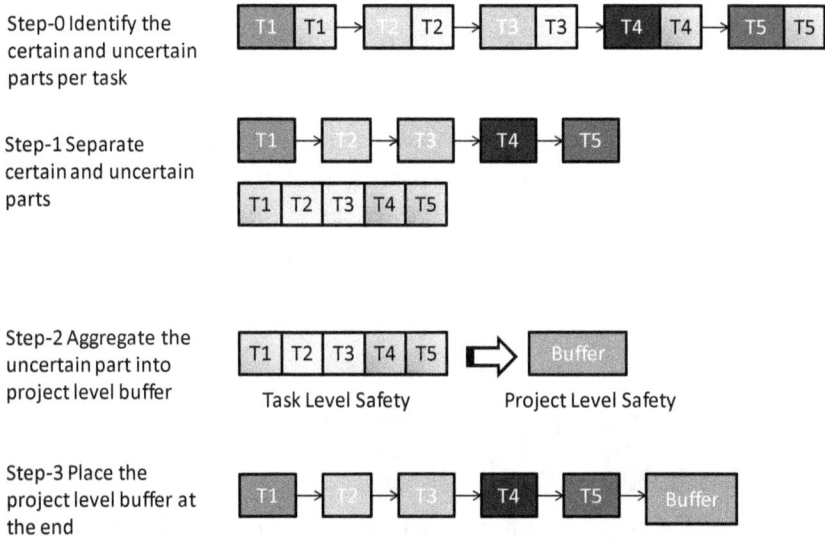

Figure 3.14: Aggregating uncertainty and placing the buffer at the end of the Critical Path provides the benefit of finishing the tasks early to the project and the necessary safety to tasks that end late, without letting the project getting late.

Neither the amount of variability at each task level, nor the certainty of variability is known. Also, when there are too many tasks in the Critical Path, all tasks will not be delayed. That is, some will complete in longer than estimated time, and some in shorter. The tasks that are completed earlier than estimated time leave the aggregated buffer unaffected. And when a particular task does get late, it has the opportunity to use not only its own safety time but also that of those finished earlier. Hence, there is logic in separating uncertainties and dealing with them separately. *The TOC solution provides more than sufficient safety at task level, yet it avoids 'project' delays.*

The beauty of scheduling a project in the TOC way is also that the safety time required at the project level is less compared to cumulative safety required by all the tasks (the Law of Aggregation).

Practitioners of TOC recommend cutting the linear sum of task safety by 50% to obtain aggregated safety (buffer) for the project. Normally, when the project buffer is placed at the end, *the project duration could reduce by as much as 25% at the planning stage itself.* So, even prior to getting into execution, the schedule of the project shrinks!

Not only the Critical Path of the project is secured by a safety buffer, any other arm of the network that feeds into the Critical Path, also has its own buffer, Figure 3.15. This protects the Critical Path from getting delayed due to any uncertainty in the feeder path.

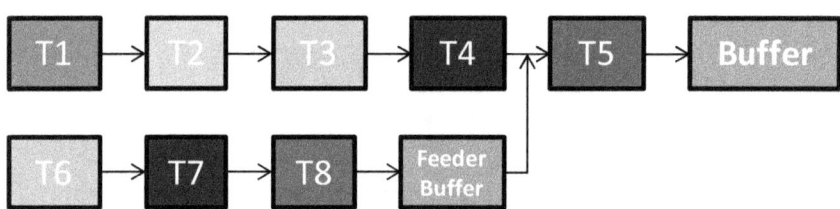

Figure 3.15: The project is also protected from the uncertainty of feeder path.

Given that people productivity is an important metric for any organization, during the planning stage, traditionally, resources are placed on multiple tasks. And often, even at the planning stage there is severe resource contention. TOC recognizes the grave danger of overlooking the impact of resource allocation and emphasizes that resource contention be liberally removed at planning stage itself, as shown in Figure 3.16, below.

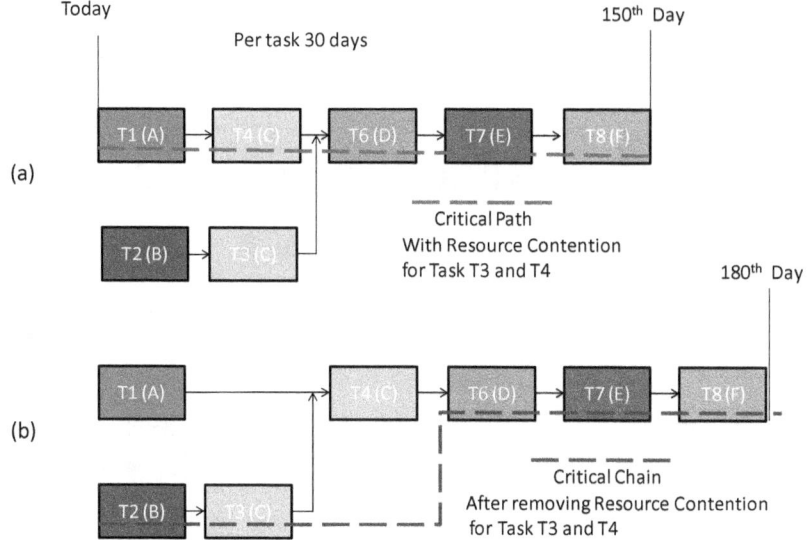

Figure 3.16 The illustration of Critical Chain

In Figure 3.16a, Tasks T4 and T3 are scheduled to take place almost in parallel by same set of resources (C). During execution this is bound to create conflict. Hence, the resources are freed of contention at planning stage itself, as shown in Figure 3.16b.

By resolving resource contention upfront, TOC makes the planning more realistic. This is in quite contrast to traditional way of planning which is centered around resource constraint and tasks are considered switched at the planning stage itself, Figure 3.17.

In fact, in traditional planning, Critical Path based on task duration, is fixed first and then resources are assigned. In TOC way of planning, resource contention is resolved and then Critical Path is identified. The new way of representing Critical Path is called Critical Chain, after which TOC's application in projects is named as Critical Chain Project Management, CCPM [4].

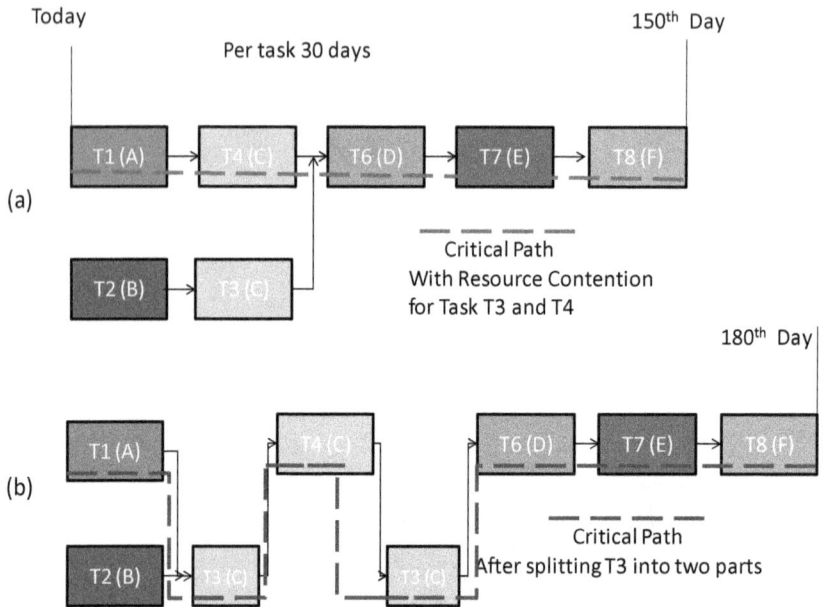

Figure 3.17 In traditional way of managing projects, resource contention is worked around by splitting the tasks that ultimately leads to bad multitasking.

Execution:

During execution of a project, the project manager must have the right information about the health of the project, so that its progression can be controlled and the project meets its promised due date. Since, the time of the project managers is precious, they should only intervene when it is required and the project buffer is in real danger. At any moment, the status of the available buffer is a good indicator of the health of the project and it lets a project manager decide when ones attention is needed.

In order to help the project manager have right indicator about the health of the project, the Buffer time is divided into 3 parts, with colors as shown in a Traffic Signal, i.e. Green, Yellow and Red. On any given day, the status of buffer is mapped on the length of buffer left to be consumed.

If on a day, the till date consumption of buffer is relatively more than progress made in the Critical Chain, then the difference is indicated as a penetration in the then allocated buffer time. If this penetration is within first 1/3 of the available buffer time, the color of the buffer is considered Green and the project does not require the project manager's attention.

Available Buffer

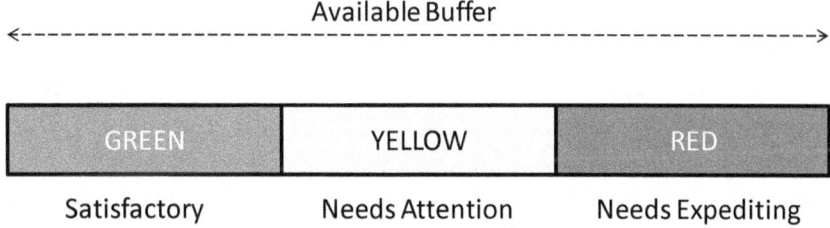

Figure 3.18 The available buffer is divided into three zones and the status of the buffer w.r.t. these three zones indicates health of the project

If on a day, the buffer penetration is more than 1/3 and less than 2/3 of the then allocated buffer time, the buffer is considered Yellow. On this day, the project manager and team start taking notice of the buffer penetration.

However, the moment the buffer is penetrated more than 2/3, it requires direct attention of the project manager and all actions are taken to expedite the project so that its buffer is retrieved to yellow or green.

As and when the consumption (penetration) of the project buffer falls into danger zone, the project manager traces back the task that is responsible for penetrating the buffer and facilitates in speeding up the task. If required the project manager may take a decision to move resources from elsewhere to expedite the project.

Further, under the TOC way of project management, resources are liberally spread and therefore, whenever a task finishes up faster (and there is always a good probability that several tasks would), with a little preparation the next task starts quickly and all other tasks are pulled ahead. The time saved is then added to the buffer, improving the probability of the project finishing not only in time but also ahead of time.

In fact, health of a project can be monitored as a trend. The project manager monitors the buffer with the progression of the project on

Critical Path. As long as the consumption of the buffer is less than the progress of the project on Critical Path, one knows that the project is under control and it does not need interference or deep review of all the tasks by the project manager.

However, buffers are built by accepting the reality that there will be uncertainty and the extent of buffer consumption compared to progress of the project on the Critical Chain would vary.

Figure 3.19 illustrates health status of the project during its lead time. Status of the project is mapped by points (stars) at different instance on the graph that shows the relative consumption of project buffer and progress of project on Critical Chain. These points are captured at different instances of reviewing the project. During the review if the status of the project on those days (R1, R4, R5, and R6) falls in the Unsafe Zone, the project team knows that it is falling behind the project timelines. This triggers necessary attention and focus on the identified tasks that lead the status of the project to Unsafe Zone. When sufficient focus is given on such tasks, the project would move into Safe Zone (points R2, R3, R6, R7, and R8) and could be delivered well in time.

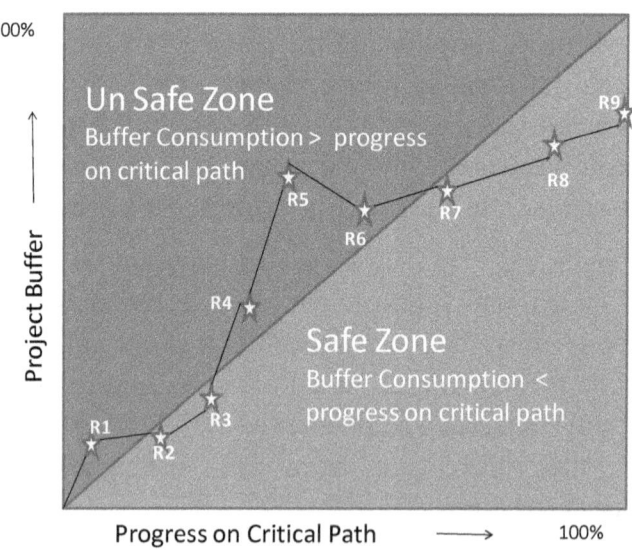

Figure 3.19 Monitoring the Project Buffer and using a simple heat chart instead of chasing task enhances project managers effectiveness and efficiency

In TOC practice, such a monitoring graph is called the Fever Chart.

Fundamentals of Effective Execution require 'Cadence of Accountability' to be followed. '4 Disciplines of Execution' [5] states that review process, called 'Cadence of Accountability' be forward looking and not based on past data. As we see in the above Fever Chart, when the project goes into Unsafe Zone, the review process can only do post-mortem and this only leads to finger pointing and blame games. In a good execution system the team must be prepared well in advance before urgency occurs.

In order to make the review process forward looking, an intermediate zone is added in the Fever Chart and is normally colored in yellow, Figure 3.20. So as soon as the project enters the yellow zone, the team starts planning for corrective actions. And if the project moves into the Unsafe Zone (Red), the team is in a position to immediately execute the plan and prevent the project from getting further late. In fact, this approach called a 'pit crew' mentality often results into innovating ways to retrieve the lost buffer.

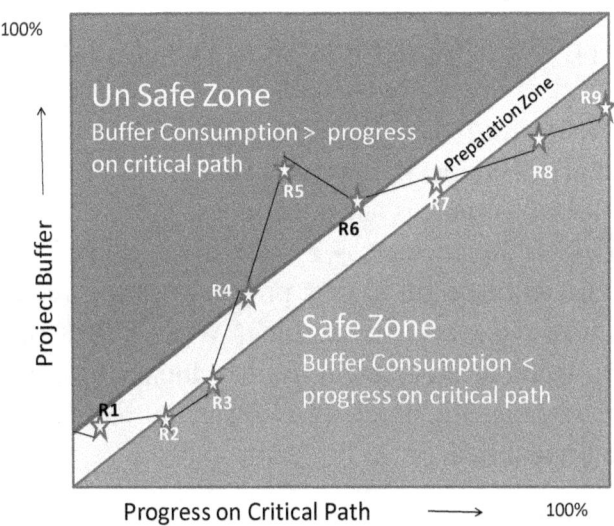

Figure 3.20 Adding a Yellow Zone (Preparation Zone) is recognition of forward looking review process.

One of the key responsibilities of the project manager is to see that Bad Multitasking is avoided. It is important that factors that contribute to Bad Multitasking be taken care of by a process. One of the reasons for Bad Multitasking is the availability of several tasks to a resource at a given time. Hence, the project manager by design must ensure that no resource is assigned too many tasks at a moment (normally two or three depending upon individual capability and organization process maturity level, are enough). Non availability of too many tasks eliminates the options for getting into Bad Multitasking. While it could be argued that this will hurt productivity, in reality the loss in project performance by allowing Bad Multitasking hurts the productivity much more than not allowing.

In a project based organization, it is a normal practice to activate (release) too many projects on the development floor at a time. As a consequence projects wait mid way for some or other reason. Now since projects are often long duration initiatives, the waiting of projects could be very long and often they wait for inputs to come from somewhere else, which could be as trivial as material, software, documents, regulatory approval, etc.

A cardinal rule in project management is that of Full Kit. This says that even if a project is due to be started, it is not released into development environment, unless it passes through an adequacy list called 'Full Kit'. Further, tasks of projects are executed on FIFO (first in first out) basis. No task is activated unless it is in front of the queue and all inputs are adequately available (Full Kitted). By following a strict discipline of full kitting, project managers reduce work in progress and avoid bad multitasking. While Full Kitting allows in reducing work in progress in the development floor, it also helps in strengthening the process of preparation needed for starting the projects and tasks.

Program Management

Within an Organization, Program Management is responsible for a number of projects of similar family of products or themes. An organization of reasonable size normally has several Program

Managers. It is their responsibility to see that *an ever increasing number of projects are finished on time in full* in their respective programs.

Program managers manage a portfolio of projects that at any time are at different stages of development, as shown in Table 3.1.

Table 3.1 Project Portfolio showing status of each project

Project ID	Concept	Requirements	Design	Development	Integration	Testing
Project-1021				■		
Project-1022						■
Project-1023					■	
Project-1024				■		
Project-1025			■			
Project-1026		■				
Project-1027					■	
Project-1028					■	
Project-1029			■			
Project-1030					■	
Project-1031			■			
Project-1032					■	
Project-1033				■		
Project-1034		■				
Project-1035	■					
Project-1036					■	
Project-1037	■					
Project-1038		■				
Project-1039	■					
Project-1040	■					
20	4	3	3	3	6	1

In a way, managing a program is like running a Plant that processes different projects, passing through different stage of development. Since time to market is the most critical parameter in Product Development function, a program manager needs to ensure that the issues that might delay projects are addressed effectively at planning as well as execution stage.

While each program has its own specialty of skills, the generic process of product development may be more or less the same. Often, there are common resources shared between projects. A program manager must ensure that projects are planned such that resource contentions are minimized and the Critical Path of projects takes care of resource contention.

The Due Date Performance of projects from Program Management point of view means that projects be released into development environment based on the committed Due Date and Length of the Critical Chain.

It must also be recognized that at any moment, the pace of product development (throughput) will be dictated by the slowest stage of the product development process. The program managers need to be aware of the slowest stage. To ensure bad multitasking, they need to ensure that new projects are released into the development floor based on the pace of the slowest process and not earlier. For example, if the integration stage made of a common team is the slowest stage, it dictates the rate at which projects can be completed in a program. Releasing projects into development floor faster than the slowest stage, would lead to increased work in progress and bad multitasking; which will result in delays and long lead time (a similar phenomenon occurs in a manufacturing plant; more WIP , more chaos, more defects, more delays etc.) In essence, a program management needs to follow certain principles of running a project 'factory' in the TOC way.

When different projects are run simultaneously within a program, projects do slip behind their milestones and often, they would need attention and facilitation from the Program Management level.

In order to not dilute ones attention, under the TOC way of executing the portfolio of projects, the program manager regularly monitors health of the respective Project Buffers.

A project whose buffer is in the danger zone takes the attention of the program manager first. A snapshot of the Operating Status of projects captured in the form of a Fever Graph as shown in Figure 3.21, helps the program manager in providing the right amount of attention to critical projects. For example, Projects P2, P4, P9, P10, P12 and P13 in the fever chart shown in the figure, have more safety eaten away than the progress on the Critical Chain and they are perhaps the most vulnerable from the view point of meeting their due dates. Thus, during execution, the Program Management becomes more effective by providing attention and facilitation to the project that needs higher attention.

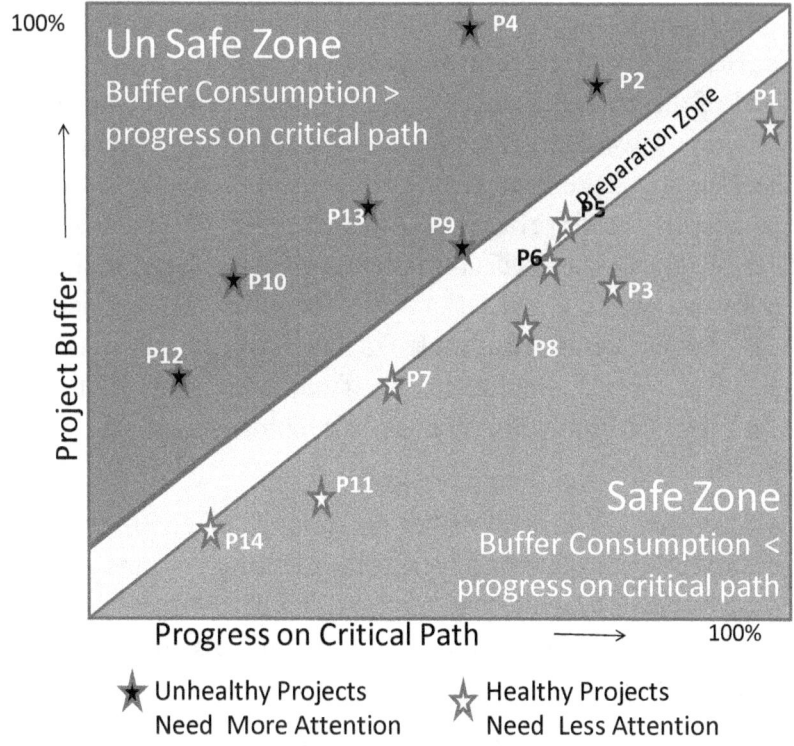

Figure 3.21 The execution stage health monitoring sheet for Program Manager

Five Focusing Steps in Project Management

Let's see how Five Focusing steps of TOC are applied to Project Management environment.

1. Identify the System Constraint (The Weakest Link):

In a single project environment, the Critical Chain (Critical Path with resource contention resolved), determines the success of the project. Hence, Critical Chain is the Constraint which prevents the project from achieving its objective of On Time completion.

In a multi-project environment the goal is to complete as many projects as possible over a time horizon. In such case, the stage of project flow that decides the number of projects delivered by the program management becomes the constraint.

2. Decide to Exploit the System Constraint (Decision Making):

First the Constraint (the Critical Chain) should be protected from any uncertainty of its not being able to meet the promised Due Date. Hence, it is decided to place an aggregated Safety Buffer at the end of the critical chain. The buffer would not only absorb the uncertainty, it would also reduce the length of the project duration at the Planning stage itself. The management then takes a decision to manage the buffer effectively. In fact, even buffers are placed for feeder lines. Also decision is taken to avoid bad multitasking by releasing projects and tasks not before they are due and full-kitted. The project team also looks into task duration and their sequence at the planning stage and if required compress the task duration by shuffling, dividing or combining series and parallel activities.

In a multi-project environment, decision is taken to maximize utilization of the constrained stage by securing its time. Further, decision is taken to avoid bad multitasking across the program by scheduling release of other projects based on the availability of the constrained stage.

3. Subordinate to the Decision to Exploit the System Constraint (Synchronized Action):

The monitoring and control of a project is based on running the complete project smoothly along the Critical Chain. It means, monitoring its performance in terms of buffer consumption and pacing the activities of the project team to the progress on the Critical Chain. Whenever, the penetration of the project buffer time is unacceptably more than the progress of the project along the critical chain, the complete project office subordinates itself to the cause of consumption of the buffer. Necessary expediting and support is provided to move the endangered task faster. It may mean calling specialists, resolving technical glitches, training the staff, placing quality control, avoiding unnecessary meetings and reviews, seeking quick external support, changing workflow, improving record keeping etc. It also means that when a task is completed well before the allocated duration, the next task is started as early as possible.

In a multi-project environment, the complete organization is aligned to protect the constrained stage. The upstream stages ensure that there is always adequate pre qualified inputs available for the constraint, while the downstream stages are always ready in a 'relay race' behavior to jump onto work as soon as a task is delivered by the constrained stage. Similarly, special consideration is provided to the constrained stage in terms of day to day staffing, training, infrastructure etc. At the same time, all available process improvement tools and techniques are employed to enhance productivity of the constrained stage.

4. Elevate the System Constraint (Capacity Expansion):

As the time passes, tasks are completed faster and there comes a time, when it becomes evident that some 'critical' tasks can't be completed within an acceptable time by the available resources or equipments jeopardizing due date performance of the project, despite all the improvement in the process. Under such a situation, resources are procured, shifts are extended, work is outsourced etc. This could occur in two instances. One, when there is a need to deliver the project much earlier than initially agreed and all the time shrink (improvement) done till then is not sufficient. Second, when it becomes clear that the project is going to be or is already too late; and existing resources and infrastructure is not sufficient.

By following Step-1 through Step-3, in a multi-project environment, excess capacity is revealed, projects finish on time, and more projects are delivered per year and per person. It reaches a stage where any further addition of projects into the development floor, deteriorates the situation. It will become evident that adding overtime, resources or outsourcing is the only way (Elevation) to crash the Critical Chain.

In a multi-project environment, the constrained stage will ultimately reach a stage where any further improvement in productivity sees the law of diminishing returns. Under such a situation the capacity of the stage is augmented by adding more people, shifts, infrastructure, new systems etc.

5. Restart the Cycle:

In a multi-project environment and in fact, in most of the manufacturing organizations dealing with multiple product developments at a time, at Program Management level, Constraints shifts from one project to another. At any moment of time, though only some projects will have their buffers in danger. As the constrained projects shift, the attention of Program Manager shifts to different projects and these projects need to follow the above four focusing steps.

When projects are rolled out like a mass production, the constraint would shift to other stages due to various reasons (e.g. complexity or project mix). Step 1-4 must then be repeated and the organization must be re-oriented to follow these steps at the new constraint.

During Step-1 to Step-4, the Project Teams and Program Managers keep collecting the reasons for delays. These delays are regularly analyzed and actions are taken to reduce their occurrences. In fact, systematic analysis of situations which make projects running into delays often give pointers to constraints outside the project environment i.e. towards organizational policies. Thus, managing projects the TOC way, just like managing the production the TOC way, unleashes a virtuous cycle of sustainable improvement culture leading to Business Excellence.

The Path to Rapid Product Development

The ongoing process of making Product Development more responsive can be summarized in following steps.

1. Static parts of the tasks, where the time durations have no variability and / or the team has no control, are identified.

2. The static parts are sequenced and scheduled.

3. Working backward from the end, the schedule is freed from resource contention.

4. The longest path of task and resource dependencies is identified to obtain the Critical Chain.

5. The estimated duration of non static part of the tasks is revised downward by 50%.

6. The revised estimated duration of non-static tasks is aggregated as common safety buffer for the project.

7. The safety buffer of the project is added at the end of the Critical Chain.

8. The safety buffer is added to all feeder paths merging into the Critical Chain.

9. Release dates for all tasks without any preceding tasks are worked backward from the promised Due Date and the length of the Critical Chain.

10. Even if a project is due to be opened for development, it is not opened if it is not Full Kitted.

11. Even if a task is due to be opened for development, it is not opened if it is not Full Kitted.

12. No project is released for development before its scheduled date of release.

13. No task is activated for development unless it is in front of the queue.

14. A new project is released into development floor only when its release is triggered by the constrained stage.

15. The project manager monitors the project by tracking the penetration levels of the buffer compared to the progress of the Critical Chain.

16. When the penetration of the available safety buffer enters unsafe zone, the task responsible for the penetration is identified and expedited.

17. When one task is under progress, the preparation for the next task is completed so that it could be started as soon as the previous task completes.

18. The time saved by starting a task early when its preceding one finishes early is added to the buffer, thus increasing the safety of the project to meet its Due Date.

19. The reasons for delays of tasks during the course of the project are regularly noted down and are systematically solved using suitable tools and methods.

20. For delays due to technical knowledge, people are trained in new methods and techniques in the domain of the project.

21. At the level of Program Management, safety buffers of portfolio projects are monitored and management attention is secured when a project turns into danger.

22. Generic reasons of delays across projects are analyzed and organizational level initiatives are launched to improve effectiveness of the overall Product Development Function.

23. When the throughput demanded from the project management office is clearly more than it can deliver, improvements are carried out at the constrained stage.

24. When the improvements at the constrained stage follow the law of diminishing returns, its capacity is augmented by adding new resources or infrastructure.

25. If the capacity of the existing stage of development ceases to be constrained, the organization must identify the stage that determines its capacity and implement the process of taking decision to exploit, subordinate and elevate the constraint.

The Realm of TOC

How is India Doing?

The Thinking Process

TOC is a focusing mechanism to achieve dramatic improvement in the performance of a system by synchronizing the organization around the Constraint. We have seen its breakthrough impact in Production and Product Development, but its impact goes far beyond these two functions.

The question we now need to answer is how TOC is applied in different functions, organizations, systems and situations. Further, the Constraint in a system is often not a Resource, under such a situation it is not a trivial exercise to identify the Constraint (the Core Problem). And then, changing the way an organization works involves dealing with people, their assumptions and behaviors. It requires a new approach to cause the change.

In order to deal with a given situation and being able to apply focusing mechanism, TOC provides a systematic Thinking Process (TP). Thinking Process equips organizations irrespective of their nature and domain, to identify and manage Constraints, and bring quick improvements, without causing costly trade-offs. It recognizes the reality that managers are required to take decisions based on imperfect and insufficient information. Thus, it helps managers in blending their intuition and experience with the available analytical tools.

When used in a systematic way, the set of Thinking Process tools, allow organizations in walking through a sequence of steps involved in establishing a sustainable improvement process. The resulting process is thus used to identify the core problem, find a breakthrough solution, build the solution, deal with obstacles, reduce the negative ramification of the evolved solution and manage the improvement program.

TOC provides a thinking tool called Strategy and Tactic Tree (S&T Tree) that connects all rationale of new solution and desired actions at the SOP levels to the objective of the organization. S&T

Tree is also a strong communication tool in allowing each layer of the organization in clarifying its understanding about the new solution, expectations and specific roles in improving the organization.

All these tools are in the form of logic diagrams and are very intuitive. It is this gamut of tools, with its own ontology that makes TOC a complete body of knowledge on improving the process of improvement. Here is the list of thinking process tools from TOC [6]:

Table-4.1 Thinking Process Tools

Thinking Process Tools	Purpose
Current Reality Tree (CRT)	Identifying Core Problem
Evaporating Cloud or conflict diagram (EC)	Resolving Conflicts and Identifying Injections (Actions And Solutions)
Future Reality Tree (FRT)	Using Injections and building a desirable Outcome
Negative Branch of Reservation (NBR)	Identifying and Trimming Undesirable Effect of Proposed Solution
Prerequisite Tree (PRT)	Identifying Obstacles and Setting Intermediate Milestones
Transition Tree (TRT)	Identify actions for Achieving Intermediate Milestones
Strategy and Tactics Tree (S&T)	Documenting and Communicating the Complete Solution from Objective to SOPs

Standard Applications of TOC

Applications of TOC are built for different situations, in Production, Project, Sales, Marketing, HR, Finance etc. These applications were originally built using the Thinking Process tools. Although, they have generic templatization for similar situations, there is always a fair degree of customization required to fit them for a particular organization. And under such situations, managers must make use of the structured thinking process to build their own process of ongoing improvement. The application discussed for the Production System is called Drum, Buffer and Rope (DBR) and the one used for Product Development is called Critical Chain Project Management (CCPM).

Table 4.2: Standard solutions from TOC

Function	Generic Applications
Production	DBR, SDBR
Supply Chain	Synchronised Pull Replenishment
Projects	Critical Chain Project Management
Marketing	Irrefutable Offer
Sales	Buy In
Finance	Throughput Accounting
Human Resource	The Thinking Process

Industry Wide Application of TOC

TOC has been applied successfully across geographies and has given enormous benefits in Manufacturing, Engineering, Construction, Health Care, Avionics, Software Development, Financial Systems, Education etc, [7]. It has been used by big as well as small organizations, by governments, by private organizations and by social organizations during growth, crisis, and peace as well as in disaster management.

If the proceedings of TOCICO conference (Theory of Constraints International Certification Organization [7]) are to indicate anything then, TOC way of ongoing improvement is at an accelerated pace across industries. Thanks to the power of TOC to give organizations 'more on less' quickly, without taking too much risk and without exhausting scarce resources.

Recorded Benefits of TOC

Application of TOC is known to give immediate benefit without exhausting costly resources and taking real risk.

As we stand today after almost three decades since Eli Goldratt introduced it, TOC has been applied in Production, Projects, Product Development, R&D and Service Business. An independent study [8] of Theory of Constraints implementations around the world found that huge results were consistently achieved, Table 4.3.

Table 4.3 Recorded benefits of TOC

Metrics	Benefits (Mean)
Lead Times	Reduced by 69%
Cycle Times	Reduced by 66%
Due Date Performance	Increased by 60%
Inventory Levels	Reduced by 50%
Revenue/ Throughput	Increased by 68%

And of course, along came significant improvement in quality and cost. *All these came in shorter timeframes, without taking too much risk and without exhausting crucial resources.* Such improvements are testimony to TOC's capability in equipping organizations in implementing improvement projects quickly, and thus dramatically improving their ability to respond faster to the changes taking place in the business environment.

TOC in India

Although TOC was not discovered in India, the Author remembers having seen copies of the book, the Goal [2] by Eli Goldratt, on the desks of Indian Production Managers in early 90s. Then, TOC was only being talked about. Starting with the new millennium, actual implementation of improvement initiatives based on TOC took off, and currently, India has reached a critical mass of TOC based improvement programs, from where it looks to pick up pace significantly. In each newer edition of TOCICO [7], the participation of Indian companies and their case studies have been growing.

Group companies of TATA, Godrej, Siemens, L&T, Mahindra & Mahindra and ABB have obtained significant benefits by implementing TOC. The companies which have found TOC way of seeking improvement very handy, within their budget, time and culture, include names like Westside, Bharat Bijlee, Fleet Guard, Crompton Greaves, Dr Reddy's Labs, Rallies, Paharpur Cooling Towers, Gokaldas Images, RDC Concrete and Liberty Shoes. These companies have obtained superlative results in lead time, inventory turns, throughput and cost, across different types of business segments.

The increasing adoption of 'the TOC way' of doing business in India, can be gazed from the fact that public listed companies have started mentioning results of TOC based projects in their Annual Reports. In fact, TMTC (Tata Management Training Centre) has made an intensive program called 'Management the TOC Way' as a standard feature of its management development program.

Buoyed by the growth prospects in India, leading experts from around the world have come together to start the Theory of Constraints Institute (TOCI) [9]. Description on its website states that it intends to empower business leaders and their teams with the knowledge, skills and tools they need to achieve breakthrough in the day-to-day operation of their business. TOCI offers seminars, workshops and advisory services designed to inspire decisive action and improve overall performance significantly. On its website, TOCI provides following typical results observed among Indian companies in a time horizon of 12-24 months:

Table 4.4 Observed benefits of TOC in India

Metric	Change
Net Sales Growth	20-50% Growth
Inventory	20-40% Reduction
Bill Receivables	10-30% Reduction
Cycle Time	2x-5x Reduction
Ontime Delivery	Shift from <10% to 90%
Stockout	From 30-40% to <5%
Project Implementation Time	20-40% Reduction
Profits & ROCE	50-200% Growth

The growing adoption of TOC in India would not have happened without the growing community of TOC practitioners and consultants. Avenir Management Service, Goldratt Consulting, Goldratt India, Mahindra Satyam, Syncore Group and Vector Consulting [10-15] represent the front league of TOC consulting groups in India. There are several small groups, individuals and freelancers, who are engaged in pushing the rate of adoption of TOC in India ahead. More recently, management schools including the IIMs have started rolling out special sessions on TOC.

The knowledge on TOC was initially created by Eli Goldratt through his popular books, and subsequently, several Authors from abroad have made significant contribution through books and publications. Presentations in TOCICO yearly conferences provide a rich library of emerging TOC concepts and case studies. The year 2010, saw the first Handbook [16] on TOC and it is perhaps, the most comprehensive reference on the subject. In a more recent development Rajiv Athavale [17 and 18] compiled a set of TOC articles from International experts in two massive reference volumes. An exhaustive list of books [19] on TOC as compiled by James Cox gives a good reference to the body of knowledge on TOC.

Although, several case studies of TOC projects in India are available on internet, an authoritative book on the application of the subject in local context is yet to be published from the subcontinent. In the knowledge of the Author, the year 2013-14 might see release of a couple of interesting books narrating TOC's application in the local environment. In fact, the year 2012 saw two sets of books on TOC released by authors from the subcontinent. 'Empowered' by Premlal Yuvaraj [20] covers the fundamental tools of TOC and their integrated application in a case study format. And then, a set of 3 e-books making Do It Yourself kit by Rajeev Athavale [21] provides a step by step approach to implementing TOC in SME sector. Both the authors have made quite an interesting addition to the knowledgebase of TOC. In fact,

Premlal Yuvaraj has gone ahead to launch e-learning platform for training professionals in TOC methodology.

In the summer of 2012, more than 100 practitioners from different industries came together to relook into the way manufacturing industries operate in India. This resulted into co-creating the first full blown book on implementation of large TOC projects in India. This book was co-created online from content to design and was placed in the hands of readers in less than 150 days. Titled, 'The Path: Leveraging Operations in a Complex and Chaotic World' [22] is a semi business novel and takes readers through the nuances of executing a large TOC project (called Viable Vision Project in TOC community).

TOC for Smarter way to Growth

Question: What is the fundamental premise on which TOC is built?

Answer: TOC recognizes that organizations operate within a resource constrained environment. And if you need to bring in rapid change, then resource elevation is not often a favorable option.

Since, Emerging Economies are inherently resource constrained, TOC plugs into their natural state, very well. Last decade, they grew at scorching pace, and a vast majority of their growth has been investment driven (read, Step-5 of Focusing Mechanism: Elevation). Under such a situation, any small disturbance in the world order of economy pushes them into despair, jeopardizing the dream of improving standard of living of their citizen (read, sustainable growth).

Being surrounded by the worst type of macro-economic turbulence, increasingly, economists and federal banks recognize that not much correction could be done by fiscal and monetary actions and presently, the situation can be improved significantly only by Execution measures. This means a higher GDP (throughput) per capita. It has, therefore, become glaringly clear *that improving productivity is the only way to achieve sustainable growth for business as well as a national economy.*

During the last two decade, India leapfrogged into a service economy without building a critical mass of manufacturing lineage. It is now threatened by an unsustainable service bubble built on weakening manufacturing base. Thanks to the New Manufacturing Policy of India, the recognition to improving manufacturing throughput and productivity is dawning upon policy makers and business leaders. Now that there is a pull in the government's vision to improve share of manufacturing in the GDP from 16% to 25% within a decade, there is an emergent need to look deeper into the way manufacturing organizations are being managed. And, it just gives a feeling that TOC could be a shot in arm for Indian manufacturers, as they strive to improve their productivity, quickly, without taking too much risk and without exhausting costly resources.

Honestly, TOC is an imperative for emerging nations to reach to the level of productivity of developed nations.

The World of Operational Improvement

Do Different Techniques Conflict?

TOC is not 80:20

Invariably, increased attention at the constrained resource drives improvement of capacity quickly, and it drives quick improvements throughout the system. In a production system, an improvement of 10% in the capacity of the Constraint (the single node in a system) means an improvement of 10% for the *entire* plant, line or flow. Thus, TOC is not about 80:20, but about an approach of 99:1, 99.9:0.1 or even 99.99:0.01. Most of the benefits from these improvements start surfacing in much earlier than one lead time. That is why TOC makes an operating system highly responsive.

Similarly, in a product development (project management) environment, it is about focusing on one thing, that is the critical chain and managing activities around it in a focused way. A complex project would have 100s of tasks. Traditionally, Project Managers monitor, review and control all these tasks and keep fighting uncertainty. When they feel the heat of fire fighting, they tend to choose the 80:20 rule, which further deteriorates the situation and saps their attention. Focusing on critical chain and controlling the project buffer let Project Managers to focus on tasks that need the most attention and achieve remarkable results.

It is important to mention here that 80:20 rules is applied when there are mutually exclusive causes or elements, i.e. when there is a clear case of independent causes to a problem. It is used in trade-off related decision makings. Once the '20' elements or causes are identified, it is possible to further drill down and identify the root cause, by 5-why technique. However, *this rule is inadequate, when the elements of a complex system or problem are interdependent*, especially when human behavior and policies come into play.

In a human dependent system, necessity and sufficiency based causality techniques, as provided in TOC, help in identifying the core problem or constraint. The (Effect-) Cause – Effect technique is not though a simple 5-why technique, rather a logic tree that relates different intermediate causes and effects to the root cause and main effect. It has a profound impact on the effectiveness of the time of managers, who often are forced to take decision based on incomplete information.

The Effect-Cause-Effect logic is used not only in identifying core problem but also in building and implementing a robust solution to the core problem through the gamut of Thinking Process tools and the related procedures.

Even when the core problem or a constraint is clearly identified, the solution or exploitation may not be directed by the 80:20 rule, for the simple reason that a constraint need not be a resource.

The Synergistic World of Improvement

There are several techniques, methods, approaches and tools to effect improvements. Each one of these tools has found good use and has benefitted businesses enormously.

On an ongoing basis, business leaders face varied situation of decision making and improvement opportunities. It is not an easy job to decide which technique is the right technique for the organization at a given moment, especially when consultants are hard selling their brainwares. Often this leads to comparison of techniques and engaging consultants into a pitched battle of comparison. Each consultant boasts advantages of one's technique and gives a proposition to solve all the problems of the organization. More than often, business leaders have no other option than to choose the technique that is presented best by the consultants.

Managers should not forget that while proven techniques are readily available for asking, their success depends on the internal capability of the organization to execute improvement projects (change).

When we talk about TOC, the comparison is often made with Lean and Six Sigma. *Actually, there is no comparison between them.*

The answer is that in the long term all lead to similar results, although they start with different issue of focus. The question is how long time and how much resources you have to deliver significant improvement. The following table places the three approaches together and as you would see, ultimately all the benefits converge.

Table 5.1 All roads lead to Rome

Criteria	TOC	Lean	Six Sigma
Objective	Improve Throughput	Improve Flow	Improve Stability
Mechanism	Manage Constraint	Eliminate Waste	Reduce Variation
Belief	One or just few elements: Constraints significantly improve performance of the System.	Many small improvements lead to overall big improvement.	Removal of variations in many places improves performance of the System.
Main Benefit	Improved Revenue	Reduced Cost	Improved Quality
Side Benefits	Improved Quality, Lower Operating Cost	Improved Throughput, Better Quality	Improved Throughput, Lower Operating Cost
Time to See Benefit	Short	Longer	Longer
Resources required	Minimal	Huge	Huge

What does this mean?

This means that there is a convergence or synergy between different techniques [23]. It may not make sense for organizations to keep sending their executives on learning each and every new technique as and when one pops up. Rather having a process that helps in identifying the technique needed to be learnt and implemented under a given situation becomes important, specifically in highly competitive business environment. It also means that the management must take the responsibility of correctly identifying the core problem, before it chooses a methodology to launch next level of improvement. The solution to the core problem must deliver significant results faster, without exhausting critical resources and without taking too much risk.

How does the synergy work?

TOC considers that ever improving revenue is the goal of a business. And this must be achieved cost effectively by delivering quality product or service. Thus the thrust is directly on Revenue and business results. Cost effectiveness (waste reduction) and Quality (variability reduction) must be achieved while improving Revenue. Thus, the direction of a good management is to focus on revenue growth, and in improving revenue whatever need to be done to reduce waste and variability must be done. TOC says that Cost Effectiveness and Quality improvement should not be confused with the goal of the organization.

We know that Theory of Constraints is a focusing mechanism. It provides a quick way to identify the weakest link in the system. Once the weakest link is identified, it provides an approach of exploiting the weakest link by synchronizing the organization around. The exploitation and subordination help in identifying the actual issues in or around the weakest link. Identification of these issues prompts the organization to deal with waste, variability or other policy issues that cause poor capacity of the weakest link. These issues are then used to identify the nature of the problem and then, systemic based problems are handled using specific techniques.

Once the weakest link is identified to have significant wastage, tools from Lean can find application to immediately give benefit to the organization. If it is found that the weakest link is highly unstable, Six Sigma can be applied at the source of variability giving a business result that would be significant and immediate.

Most often the resource itself may not be the weakest link by its own design and way of operation, although it may seem to be. However, the weakest link will give indication towards other places in the organization, where the waste needs to be eliminated or variation needs to be reduced. It would also happen that in certain cases, the weakest link may not be chronic and would shift places in short time (wandering constraints). It then becomes important to find the reason for the wandering constraints... and it could be the demand variation, the release policy, man power allocation policy, poor quality, unstable process, skill sets etc.

This means that we need to reduce waste, reduce variability, correct unsuitable policies, restructure the organization to the current business conditions, improve skills levels of human resource, improve quality of maintenance, improve yield, improve flexibility etc, but for doing any of these on standalone basis across the organization would be overwhelming and it would exhaust management attention too early. Using TOC to know when and where to cause these changes will help giving faster improvement, without taking too much risk and without exhausting costly resources.

Where to Begin

3 Hints

Surfacing 20% Hidden Capacity in less than 30 hours

October 2011, Kolkata

The Trigger

Abhijit Sarkar had sent a copy of the manuscript of my book, 'The Path' [22], to Jayant Sen the Chairman of Infaproducts, a well established Multi Product Company. Jayant Sen found the description of the problem very accurate and the reading very smooth. He recommended Abhijit to have the book on every executive's desk.

After a few weeks, Abhijit called me and said, "Jayant Sen is my very close friend and he wanted me to check with you, if you could come down to Kolkata and do a survey of his company."

I did not understand much of the need, but assured him of a meeting with Jayant Sen soon. A couple of days later... Abhijit called back and pressed urgency to meet Jayant Sen.

Description of the Situation

Incidentally, Jayant Sen came to Bangalore and requested me to accompany him to Kolkata. I realized his urgencies.

During over 2 hour flight, he told me, "Sir, I can identify four big problems."

And then, read out from his pocket diary.

"First: Utilization of our equipments is very poor; it is 30-35 %."

"Second: People take daily targets, but do not meet even 60% of their commitment."

"Third: There are too many people in the Plant; we have 256 contract workers out of a total of 509."

"Fourth: Our costs are high; we need to bring our costs down."

He continued, "Sir, it seems that we have fallen into a vicious cycle."

I clarified, "I see. But these are not problems. These are description of the situation you landed into, or say, symptoms."

And then, asked, "What do you think the real problem could be?"

He looked at me and said, "People say that often materials are not available and sometimes, the available people are not enough. In fact, it is the latter reason that has led to addition of contract employees."

Then, He said, "We have actually two plants. The first plant meets our today's market requirement. The second plant is newly built and is due to undergo a statutory audit for Developed Markets. It will be productive in another year or so. In fact, it has taken a lot of our attention and money. And it is placing more pressure on us and making us look deeper into operating cost of the first plant."

I listened to him and then said thoughtfully, "So, the company is not able to achieve its Goal i.e. to make money. And it is running out of cash and perhaps, its working capital is seemingly ballooning."

"Indeed!" he acknowledged his deep rooted worry.

Later on, I asked him, "How many products do you have?"

He said, "May be 300."

I said, "So around 1200 SKUs".

He said, "May be more than that, because we send a whole lot of products to African and Latin American countries, and each country has its own packaging requirement, in addition to some special quality parameters and features."

Infaproducts is active in India and abroad. It is into branded and white label products. It is proud of its Quality. In fact, Jayant Sen said, "We started in late 1960s, and since then, we have been focusing on Quality. Our products require very high degree of quality levels; both our customers and several reputed third party

Auditors are involved in qualifying our products. We have a very favorable positioning in the Indian market for the quality of our products. Perhaps, it is because of our 'quality first' attitude, we have not looked deeply into productivity. "

I said, "Of course quality is a boundary condition to qualify in today's market."

He explained further, "Around 20% revenue comes from white labeled products that are exported, while 80% comes from branded products. But the fact is that the 20% white label products take 80% of our capacity, effort, money and time."

I said, "Aha...!"

Then, I asked a dumb question, "Why do not you manufacture more of branded products and less of white label Products? You will make more money!"

"You know, after being in branded products for a long time, we need to look for future and build ourselves into white label products, where the future game will be played. We are still new into white labels. We need to break in there. We can't avoid expanding into new markets." Jayant Sen said in a determined tone. In fact, he also headed marketing function.

And then, he said, "Sir, we want you to conduct a survey in our plant and know if our costs are justified."

So, there was a lure of future Revenue from abroad and the frustration of the money locked in the building of a new plant for the Developed Market. I realized the chaos the company would be into. I wished to help Jayant Sen, but wanted to avoid taking a broom and becoming a cleaner of all the muck around. Also, he came with certain deep rooted assumptions, where his focus was shifting towards cutting cost; and employees seemed to be cost elements. There would also be certain more assumptions amongst his managers. Somewhere, the focus seemed to have shifted from making money to saving money.

I did not wish to make a survey of his operations and leave his team with a proposal of consulting assignment. I wanted to see that the team understands the reality, recognizes its limitation, sets the right direction and gets into action mode than chasing me for a solution to their problem.

Urgency and Emotions

The next day morning, Jayant Sen came along with his Son-in-Law and Director, Tapas to pick me up at the Park Hotel. We drove towards the Plant, some 30 kilometers away, in the outskirts of the city.

On the way, Tapas said, "We have big problems. Our operating cost has more than doubled in one year. The energy cost is up by three and half times, we have just been adding people almost everywhere. Ratio of external to internal staff is now over 1:1 from 1:3 within a year. But the production has not increased. Compared to last year, we are far behind in throughput numbers."

Tapas paused for a while, and then, said, "Every time, we ask for higher production, there is a demand for more manpower. Whenever we provide manpower, there would be so many other reasons to justify why the numbers planned on the day are not achieved. Now, we do a ten day plan and closely monitor the production. But we get only 50 percent of the day's planned output. When there are so many problems brought to us, we are not in a position to say anything. Things seem to be going out of hands. Utilization of our equipments is less than 30 percent and compared to industry average figures, our conversion cost is more than double. We need help."

He took his handkerchief, wiped his lips and asked, "Sir, what is your experience, if our productivity is really low and whether our number of contract staff is justified?"

I had no answer to this question. Looked like they came thoroughly prepared, but in the wrong direction, or perhaps, were reeling out what they could comprehend. They were expecting me to say in

"Yes or No" and give my expert comment, so that they could ask their HR manager to start cutting the flab.

I said in a reflective mood, "It is very difficult to find another company of the same revenue level, and if we find one, the portfolio of products and complexity of the production flow may not be the same. It is futile to compare with others. However, 30% average utilization is a norm in your industry. I think that it is not the challenge of the huge number of people. The right question to ask is, 'where do we have more people and where less.'"

As Jayant Sen kept thinking, Tapas said, "But there still be some reference numbers."

I said, "Yes, we will get it; but whether it is cost, number of people or any other performance indicator, your current level of performance would be because of the way you operate your plant, which is not same as the way others do. Hence, you need to take a deep look into the way the plant operates and *figure out what prevents it from getting more revenue.* May be that you try to achieve more revenue per employee by increasing revenue than cutting cost or reducing number of people."

It probably did not go so well with Tapas, as he said, "But we can't operate at such a low utilization and with so many people, when the revenue is so low." Later, he said that the rapidly changing and increasingly unpredictable market conditions were putting additional pressure on him.

I realized the emotions and frustrations that were about to hit the discussion, and said, "Let's get into details and see what causes these undesirable effects." I knew myself that I am not comfortable *a priori* fixing a decision on actions to be taken to reduce cost.

The Big Expectation
We reached the Plant in about 60 minutes. We walked into the conference room. As we entered, the team rose up and we introduced ourselves. Finance, Production, Supply Chain, Sales, HR and Planning teams were already in the room and were going through a presentation.

After we took the seats, Jayant Sen spoke about the status of the company and the key pain points which he had given me a brief about. Then, he introduced me to the team.

He requested me to give a bit more information about my work. I had accumulated a lot of operational experience during past decade and had enough details gathered about Infaproducts. I connected the two, and emphasized the need of moving ahead in a way that reduces the time it takes to cause the organizational change, without taking too much risk and without exhausting costly resources.

Thereafter, The CFO, Kunal Basu stood up and projected the presentation from his Laptop.

The header slide of the presentation carried my photograph and a formal welcome message. On the next slide a cryptic sentence from my website was captured that said, "*Revealed 20% extra capacity of key products for a leading multi product company within 14 days*". This slide made their expectations very clear. It put me under pressure, but I thanked them.

You must realize that when you just walk into a new customer and you are asked about the benchmarks, direct answers and solutions, your opinion; and an expectation of repetition of your past experience, without getting any prior detailing or investigation... you are not just in a tough situation....you are in a rather sensitive situation because the customer is emotional, desperate and seeking help.

Problems a Plenty
The next slide contained flow of the presentation. There were bullet points about the background of the company, history, size, growth story, improvement programs, specializations, honors, products, geography.... and the problems.

Kunal went through the next few slides one by one, which I felt was a thoroughly prepared presentation. In the beginning, I gave sometime to myself and the team, by asking general questions that most of the people would ask in a presentation like this.

There was a slide on issues faced by the company which seemed to have been prepared after a lot of discussion. I spent some time in understanding them. *Some* of these issues are shown in Figure 6.1 below.

The list consisted of many different things; the team stated that it did not know how to handle so many, and many more issues which keep on surfacing on day to day basis. It said that the company was seriously trying to improve the situation, but when one issue was solved, other would pop up; when the other was resolved the first one would reappear at a different location, on different product. The team said that it had fallen into a 'Vicious Cycle'.

Jayant Sen had in fact, used the phrase, 'Vicious Cycle' during our discussion in the airplane. The phenomenon of "Vicious" cycle is explained in great details in the book, 'The Path - Leveraging Operations in a Complex and Chaotic World' [22]. It is a situation from where, the current knowledge and capabilities of the team is not sufficient, to fish it out.

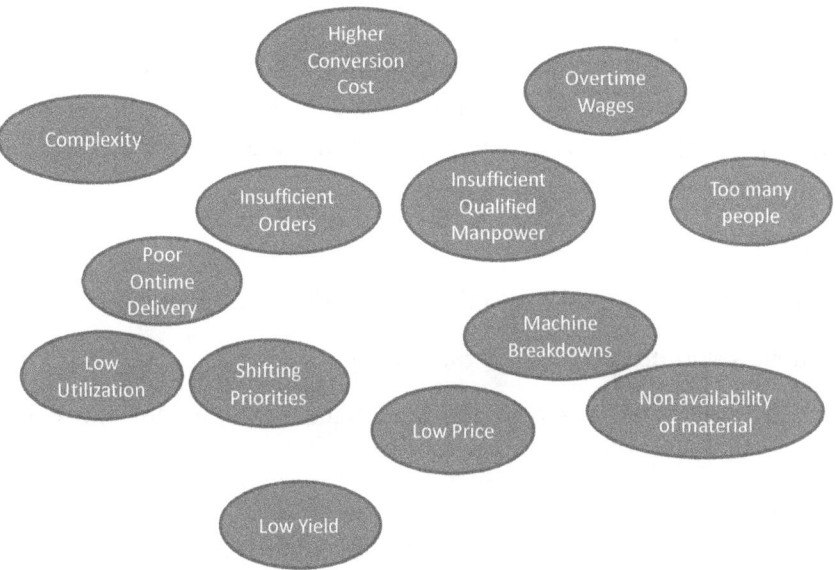

Figure 6.1: A set of issues faced by the Plant, (there were, though, a minimum of 30 issues)

The Export Manager, Manas Ganguly said, "Sir, this is the senior management team and all of us have been with the company now for almost 10 years. We have made great strides, but now we feel that making improvements in any direction is not leading to any effective results. We are demoralized since things are not moving much, despite all escalation and *expediting*. We do not know why, because there are so many things on our table. We get regular increments in our pay, because our owners are good, but we hate our individual growth when the company is not moving up. There is enormous pressure on cost. Yes, we have fallen into a vicious cycle." This was another indication of emotions and goodness of people!

After looking at the list, three issues were very clearly identified, which were from those, Jayant Sen and Tapas had briefed me about.

In recognition of their good preparation for the meeting, I said, "Very good."

Identifying the Right Metric

My practice in Business Model Innovation, where I am involved in improving the logic of business, forced a reflexive compulsion to start from customer end. And I picked up one issue, the 'Poor On Time Delivery'.

I asked, "Is On Time Delivery really an issue?"

And then said, "I think, I need to talk to the sales team."

Manas stood up in a jerk, "Yes, it is!"

Jayant Sen, who was also the lead marketing guy for the team, said, "Yes, it is a big problem."

Then, Manas said, "Today we promise 60 days delivery time, and are never able to meet the committed due date. Our..."

Anup Das, the Plant Manager interrupted, "But we are always able to supply, whatever they want."

Jayant Sen said, "No, this is definitely a problem, we have difficulty in retaining the customers and in growing our volume, only because of this issue." And Anup Das kept quiet.

"OK, one question, if we improve our On-time Delivery, do you think we can get more customer orders?" I asked.

"Of course… yes. Actually our lead time is too long, I don't know, may be 120 days. Some of our competitors, small as well as big are able to supply within 45 days of lead time. I am sure they bluff but they can't do so for a long time," said Manas.

"But we never got such a feeling, we have always stretched ourselves to deliver everything sales asked for…Often, we do not have raw materials on time and we have to wait for containers to be filled before we ship, which sometimes cause delays." Anup Das did not seem like the guy who would keep quiet.

Kunal who owned the management information system, said, "Anup, you do not know about delays because everything is behind schedule. So measurement of On Time Delivery is not being done for quite some time." It indicated how the team had resigned to live with the vicious cycle.

I got up, walked towards the white board, lifted the marker and wrote, "Prime Metric #1: On Time Delivery, OTD".

"We need an opinion and this is extremely important. We know that competitors offer 45 days lead time, while we offer 60 days. And if we are not able to do in even 60 days… and in all probability, we are in the band of 90-120 days, is On Time Delivery an important measurement for us. And if we improve it, will we make more money?" I placed emphasis on the last sentence.

Raising pitch of my voice, I said, "Yes," and lifted my right hand in affirmation.

Everybody in the hall lifted right hands, including Anup Das, his production staff and even the Admin Manager. Some people bent their left shoulder down to lift their right hand as high as possible. I looked at Anup Das and raised my right eye brow in amazement; he took it sportingly and nodded with a smile.

I encircled the phrase, 'On Time Delivery', and said, "Let us accept 'On Time Delivery' as a Prime Business Metric, and find a way to improve this dramatically. This is a good parameter to chase. Any improvement that we do will be worth an improvement if it improves On Time Delivery. Yes!!!"

"Absolutely!" said Tapas, who was vigorously taking notes.

The presentation quickly moved over to numbers that started pointing towards problem areas. I did not have to ask too many questions because others were seeking explanations on the numbers, their source, the calculation, etc. It helped me to know their terminology, the numbers, the issues and most importantly, who were getting affected by the numbers.

When emotions started boiling up on business issues and directionless frustrations became apparent, I knew that I was getting into a familiar ground.

I had to get up occasionally, because everybody was pounding on Anup Das and his team, and he was defending with all his might, why something was seemingly on the wrong side.

Every time Anup Das was cornered, he would say, "Actually this priority...this decision... this plan... was discussed in Director's meeting. It was approved by Tapas... and we did as we agreed ..."

He would say, "Sir you are my boss...you are the owner... I have to listen to you...." And he would fold his hands. I would see the owners helpless and the conference hall would come to a standstill.

I would continue to intervene and calm down the crazy discussions. The team would talk about different orders, products, consignments and people; and open up the complete history of the plant naked.

At one moment, I found that Anup Das was almost about to get into a fiery argument, I interrupted and said, "We need to take a break here, please understand that there seem to be so many different reasons why things would get delayed. And believe me, everybody in the team is making huge effort to avoid these delays, otherwise there is no reason why you would stay together for past one decade. The very reason that you are so intensely emotional in your discussion, shows how much you care about the organization, and how much you want to improve the situation. You are doing your best."

Then, I said, "It is not about questioning technical or functional expertise of any body. There are too many variables and we often turn to reacting to events caused by variability. And therefore, we keep on getting newer and newer problems, in different hues and colors. We must understand that thus far, the organization has reached to this level of growth, only because of the capability of the people. However, now the organization is not able to grow the same way because its capabilities are challenged much more than it could take in. We need to accept that variability is enemy number one and deal with it, rather than remotely recalling some past events and trying to attach a reason to it. It will not help. .... Which means that our capability to deal with variability needs to be enhanced."

"Yes… Yes, you are absolutely right. There may be problems in different functions. But the big problems that are often causing heartburns and demoralization move from function to function. And nobody is able to predict when it will occur, where it will occur and how long it will stay," said Tapas.

I continued, "Let's understand it better. Some variability is caused by external factors, while others by internal ones. When these variabilities occur they appear in different ways in front of us at different point in time as their effects or symptoms. Since, we are not conscious about the phenomenon of variability, we tend to react to the events, which might have caused by some action at some other point in time at some other place, for our supply chain is very long and our response time is over 120 days. It is our responsibility to improve our capability to deal with variability by understanding the complete chain of events, and not just one isolated event. Agreed!" I knew that I was coming close to exposing them to some basics.

"Agreed!" said Jayant Sen.

Changing the Direction of Thinking

I took a can of aerated drink, sipped through, and said, "Before we move ahead from here, I want to explain one thing and we must consider it seriously for our discussion here onwards. Jayant Sen started this company 40 years back, with an engineer, a supervisor and a few technicians. He then added products, built infrastructure, created suppliers, built customers, entered into new markets and now, today you are an organization complete from suppliers to customers. This was the process of building an organization. But when we talk about its performance and operations, we have to move in the opposite direction i.e. we must look at the market, customers, products, delivery chain, plant and suppliers. This is a very important shift in the outlook. Which means that all actions taken in the company and in the plant have to be traced back from customers and not the other way. Is this clear?"

"OK," said a few voices.

Whenever, I give this logic, it places extremely heavy pressure on people's mind and compels them to think in a counter intuitive direction. I stopped for a while and paced the room, to allow the comment to sink into the room.

"Yes, very important point. The way we currently operate is in the wrong direction," Tapas made a strong comment.

"Yes, today we try to *push* things, and therefore, delays and mismatches," quipped Manas.

I said, "This is the way for the team to link, as well as improve its performance to revenues which comes from the market. All actions must be based on what promise you make to the market. There are aspects of new products, which we will talk later."

I concluded, "And therefore On Time Delivery becomes very important, if customers are measuring us by that."

Jayant Sen said, "Yes, if customers are measuring us by OTD, we can't have a different parameter. We must measure ourselves by the *Pull* from the market."

OTD was thus, agreed as a parameter of supreme importance. The challenge was now how to improve it.

Often Poor Utilization of Plant is a Serious Concern

A flashy slide about the utilization of equipments and people appeared on the screen. It displayed area-wise utilization of the Plant and the allocated number of people. And, there were the respective average utilization numbers.

I always have a problem in looking at numbers in so many places, it confuses and diffuses attention.

The CFO, Kunal said after explaining the spreadsheet, "Utilization of our equipments is 30%. The utilization of our costliest machine is less than 25%. This is a gross negligence... people do not know worth of our assets."

There was again an emotionally loaded discussion on why some equipment was ordered, how the product mix changed and why utilization became low. The faces of the Owners (Jayant and Tapas) were turning pinkish red, as they felt that they believed in people competencies and allowed investment but people were not making use of the investment. The ROI was very bad.

Tapas looked at Jayant Sen and shook his head in denial.

Before the hall could again turn cacophonous, I intervened.

I got up and said, "The utilization can be low, and the average number that you are projecting is not far away from several other plants. I am not saying that this is good or even acceptable average utilization. But we must see it in terms of market demand and not in isolation. Sometimes, there is no demand on certain machines, while at other times, there is high demand. The plant wide average is bound to be much lower than designed capacity. This is natural."

I felt the stretch in my voice, "However, since the average utilization has remained at the same level for years and recently, we have been producing lower volumes means that perhaps, we have hit a flow blocker, somewhere. Again, we can have a number of reasons if we go work order by work order, trying to find out why the utilization is low. But as I said earlier, that is not the right way. We need to find a way to identify the root cause; and believe me there would not be many root causes, although I can guarantee that for the same symptom there would be not 10, not 12 but more than 30 intermediate reasons. Right now, the root cause is eluding us because we do not have the capacity to see it. We will need to find a way to identify it. And the best way is to start from the market."

Long Tail is Here to Stay

Then, Kunal projected a filled in template which I had provided him to capture Product details. I asked him to sort the data with respect to Revenues.

The top 10% products contributed to 80% of sales. And then there were products that were contributing to less than 0.01% of sales.

I asked them, "How easy it is to supply these tiny products?"

"This is one of the reasons, why our productivity is low. We are asked to produce less than 50 pieces of some bloody SKU, for which the process time is a few hours but the change over time is over a day. And therefore, the utilization is low." Anup jumped in with confidence, as soon as he got an opportunity. He made an important point though.

"Not only this, even our dispatch containers wait for long time when these products are in production," said the FG Warehouse Manager.

"We often pay heavy demurrage for these products as their orders are often picked on committed and competitive due dates." Manas revealed.

"How is the profitability of these products…?" I asked.

"It is very low, for many it is negative..." Kunal said in a long stretched tone.

"Why do they exit?" was my innocent question.

"Some 10 years back, we had entered the export market as per a major strategic policy. While Africa and Latin America continue to be the underserved markets, we have continued to push new products to build big enough basket of offerings and build the base." Tapas said, while defending the decision.

"Good! A very good reason indeed. The decision taken some 10 years back was right for the situation and assumptions of that time. Now looking at today's situation, we have some learning from our experience. And the experience is that the Long Tail is dramatically...dramatically reducing our back end capability." I said. I drew the Long Tail graph showing a highly inverted and lopsided relationship between Sales and Number of SKUs.

Manas accepted, "Yes, I must accept that we over stretched the tail and it has created a lot of complexity across the system."

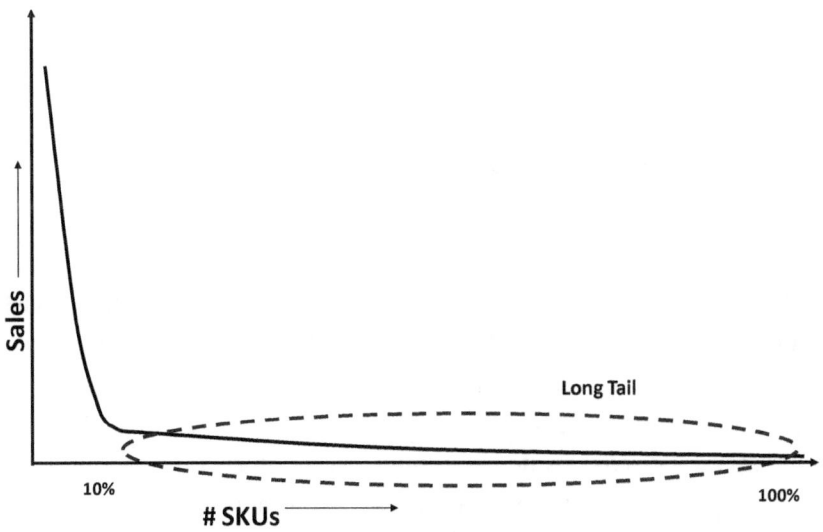

Figure 6.2 Long Tail is rapidly becoming inherent characteristics of the Industry.

"Yes, complexity and therefore.... A lot of *variability... Our enemy number one*. We need product variety but not so much that it works negatively for the organization."

I clarified, "Please understand, I am not saying that the Long Tail in absolute terms is too complex. But the current size of the 'Long Tail' of our portfolio is too complex for 'our current capability' to manage it. May be that in another six month time, if we improve our capabilities to deal with variety and variability, this Long Tail would be manageable with higher profitability."

"Which means that we need to restrain the tail to match optimally to our 'current capability'," said Kunal in a hurry.

"Yes, may be for the time being, but ultimately, we will need to get back to this, for which we need to improve our utilization," said Jayant Sen, sipping tea from the gold rimmed cup.

The realization that indiscriminately building portfolio lowers the overall capability of the organization dramatically, was very profound. That the Chairman and the Export Manager were also concerned about undesirable effects of the tail was a big relief to the team.

"Shall we take action point #1 as Rationalization of the Long Tail?" I asked.

"Yes, and put it on me," said Jayant Sen as he took the accountability to deal with the menace. I was amazed to see the readiness of Jayant Sen to take up the charge.

I was very cautious about this decision and repeated, "Please understand that we are not cutting the tail. In today's competitive world, the Long Tail is now a characteristic of most of the Industries. But 'currently' the tail of our portfolio is too long for our capability. Now since it would take some time to build this capability, we want the portfolio to be rationalized so that we can reduce the uncertainty, variation and noise, and be more effective in improving our capability quickly. Once we do that, we will bring back the tail and may be a longer one."

"And the way to rationalize the tail is to look deeper into the portfolio and classify products against a set of criteria. In any case, we need a process in place that on an ongoing basis keeps the tail matching to our abilities."

"Sure, we will start on this immediately." said Manas.

Agreement on the Process of Improvement
I was satisfied that thus far, things went well.

Jayant Sen said, "Looks like we need to change ourselves on looking at things differently. By looking at things the way we are used to, we may not be able to see some things that are important and fundamental."

Then he said, "Probably, we are missing some pattern in the problems and the obvious solution."

After a while, I said, "In fact, solutions to the large number of problems exist within this team and I can bet on this." I saw people awe-stuck for a moment.

I repeated, "The solutions to the problems exist within the team. It is different that we are not able to see exactly where to apply respective solutions."

"You mean that we are not able to pin point the core problem," asked Anup Das.

I said, "Exactly... Most prevailing approaches of business improvement tell that an organization comprises a number of parts and improving every part improves business. This means that addressing so many different problems daily will improve its performance. However, we know that it only dilutes our attention and exhausts our efforts. This way of identifying and solving the problem is not useful in a competitive world."

"Actually, the flow of products from the plant to the market passes through a chain of activities that are interconnected. The flow of our products and therefore, the throughput and revenue is decided by the *weakest link* in this chain. It follows the analogy that strength of a physical chain is decided by the strength of the weakest links (leverage points)."

Figure 6.3 Strength of the Chain is decided by the weakest link.

Since business is a living *system* comprising several *interconnected building blocks*, at any moment its growth would be limited by just *a few leverage point(s)*. I wanted to take the team's confidence in not trying to correct everything but attacking the leverage point. And the resulting quick benefit is obtained without exhausting their costly resources and without taking too much risk. I needed to take them along a methodology to demonstrate the power of leverage point.

I proposed, "What I can do now is, provide a methodology that can lead us to *identify the leverage point*, and then I would need your experience to devise a solution."

"Agreed!"

"Agreed!" said the team in disbelief.

"So where do we start from?" I asked blindly.

"We must start from the market." Said Kunal-the CFO, he had certainly got hooked onto the right direction of thinking.

"Ok." Then looking at Manas, I said, "Manas, can we identify at least one product, for which if we improve delivery time and throughput, you can sell it immediately, without any sales overhead."

"Of course yes, there are quite a few." He said.

"But I want only one, so that we can quickly demonstrate a process to identify huge scope of improvement for the overall business." I insisted.

"Sure," said Manas.

Then I said, "Do one thing, look at your portfolio of 200 products, decide a few criteria for selection and let me know which product you choose."

Manas looked at Kunal, who said, "Let's spend some time on this, immediately after the lunch."

Then Kunal asked while looking at me, "Sir, what are the next steps from here."

I said, "We are going to pick this one product, and trace it back from market into the plant, and then to the one point that prevents it from being produced more. Subsequently, we will have a process in place to see how we can deal with the Flow Blocker. It should not take much time and by tomorrow morning, we will have a decision on where to apply *improvement activities*."

I added, "By the time you guys identify the product, I would like to go inside the Plant and have a quick walk through. Upon returning, we will get all the things required to spot the Flow Blocker. It should not take us more than a couple of hours."

"That's fine," said Kunal.

"Let's then finish our lunch, before you go inside the plant," said Tapas.

We got up from our chairs, Jayant Sen walked up to me and said, "Sir, I would be leaving in the afternoon, but everybody else would be here for anything you need."

Then, he instructed his team to hang on there, till whatever time it takes.

We went to the executive lounge. The lunch was simple and we again introduced ourselves more about our families, cities and lives. It was very friendly environment. It was so nice to know people at individual levels and share our network of contacts.

Walking Thru the Plant

I returned from the lunch and walked towards the Plant along with Anup Das. We walked into his cabin, where he briefed a little about the capacity of the Plant. He gave me a dope on the high quality levels and the sophisticated processors they had. Then, he walked me into the Plant.

We entered from the visitor gate. I was given a new shoe, a brand new apron and a helmet.

We entered the material release area, although I would have preferred to start the walkthrough from the FG Warehouse end. I talked to the young man there, who Anup Das introduced as their current Kaizen King. I looked at the release plan. It was a 10 day plan that showed which batch was to be run on which machine across the plant including the Gating operations. Anup Das explained that they divide the month into 3 parts of 10 days each, and the planner circulates the list of schedule to everybody to follow.

I looked at the list and asked the young man, "How many orders are to be released today."

He counted and said, "Sir, 15 orders."

"How many are released so far."

He said, "Three."

"Why three?"

"Sir, some materials are yet to be cleared by QC."

I said, "I see."

Then, I asked him to tell me the number of orders released the day before as compared to the plan. There were tick marks against the process orders and he said, "Four out of fourteen."

"I see," I said.

Anup Das, then took me across the warehouse and explained the sophisticated raw material tracking system. It was impressive.

He gave me a set of safety goggles and said, "Sir, we are entering into the process area."

I wore the goggles and entered into the Gating Operation area. Inside the area, he took me to a large complex machine comprising several arms and digital readouts, and said, "Sir, this is our 500 processor, the most sophisticated equipment. We have stopped using traditional ones, that were less efficient and cumbersome to use."

I looked at it and smiled. He wanted to explain about it more, but before he could, I said 'hello' to people working there.

Anup Das said, "We have another processor that would come in this space." He pointed to the empty space in the room.

He took me into two more Gating Operation areas. Then, I insisted him to show me the place where the semi processed components are stored.

We walked up to the first floor, to an intermediate storage room. The room was locked and he instructed the nearby gentleman to open the door. In a while, the gentleman came back with keys and quickly opened the room.

I asked him, "How many batches do we do in a day?"

He said, "Sir, around fifteen."

I asked, "How many batches do we have here?"

He pointed to the wall, where a white board hung, and description of batches was neatly listed in red ink. The gentleman said, "Sir, it is 18."

I asked, "Are these the only intermediate batches?"

The gentleman said, "Sir, we have another small place."

I said, "I want to see that place."

Anup Das said, "Sir it is on the other side of floor. Let's complete this zone and we will go there later"

I said, "OK."

Then, we walked into the Shaping area. A pretty clean room with machines running smoothly. The team there, as if ready for discussion, showed me the variance table of key parameter and explained how they improved quality of products by following Kaizen. I realized that the team in the plant was very strong in using tools of Lean and TQM.

We moved through several other Shaping areas. To me all looked the same, some running slower, while others running faster.

Then, we walked through the Finishing area and moved over to packing lines. Anup Das explained about the innovation they had done to see that machines were simpler to work. He explained about some technicalities why they had particular type of machines and how they were debottlenecking another machine to increase productivity by 50%. I listened intently.

In the meanwhile, I asked him to take me to the finished intermediate area. He took me to two rooms that had together around 30 batches waiting for packing.

In the packing area, just around 1/3rd of the machines were working. On the secondary side, there was a crowd of people busy entering primary packed products into cartons. The manager explained me that for the type of packing and size of products, they do manual packing. They do not have Cartonators (which insert products into Cartons automatically) because they cost a lot and have disruption issues. I listened.

He then took me to the FG warehouse… and I was already tired… When we entered, I could not see end of the walls of the room from which ever angle I looked at. I bent my head to see along the walls, but in all directions I could only see hundred of shippers spread across a space almost half the size of a hockey field, filled in all three dimensions. Anup Das told me how they were trying to move things safely and quickly out from the warehouse and the new conveyor system they were implementing to directly shift the cartons onto the truck. I listened.

Anup Das then started talking about the continuous lines and the innovation they had done to increase productivity. I was not interested in getting into details here. And, requested him to walk back to the conference room.

Anup Das was too much enthusiastic and took me around a few more workstations. I requested him that we had very little time and people must be waiting for us to take the discussion further.

He took an about turn and we walked back towards the exit door of the plant. On the way, Anup Das continued his story of Kaizen and the awards they had won in the regional quality competitions..

The intensity of our discussion and the effort spent on managing team during the morning session took a lot of my energy. And then, the walk through inside the plant with heavy boots and head covered with helmet, tired me out.

Tracing the Leveraged Path

After we returned to the conference room, I went and washed myself to get a bit water into my body. I was perhaps a bit dehydrated and contrary to my belief that day in Kolkata was a bit warmer.

I walked back into the room. Tapas, Kunal, Manas and the team were busy running through the product list.

And I enquired, "Are we ready?"

Manas said, "Yes."

I asked, "So which product do we choose?"

They looked at an XL™ sheet, showed me customer-wise sales numbers ... I understood their dilemma.

I asked them to filter them in the order of sales and directed them to pick up the top most products.

They chose one, and then I asked them about the next product and the next product... I wrote names of these products on the whiteboard along with their share of the sales of the company. Top 10 products had actually contributed 95% margins from the recent sales.

I asked them, "Which one we must pick, such that if the delivery and throughput are improved, we will be immediately able to sell and add the margins to the bottom-line."

They chose one with 12% market share. And then, analyzed margins, ease of sale, customers, future potential etc. During these discussions, I facilitated them in identifying 6 criteria for choosing their key products which needed their attention. Subsequently, they realized that they would not like to bet on the chosen product, rather on another product that already had a waiting demand in the market and so, they zeroed the one with 9% of the total sales.

I advised them to quickly make a single page policy document listing the criteria for the selection of Leveraged Products. They agreed to hold a discussion the next day with relevant people to build a policy document that would help them in picking key products for critical decision making situations.

Tracing Leverage Point inside the Plant

I encircled the product name, drew four boxes and named them Gating, Shaping, Finishing and Packing. And then asked, "Is this the process, the product goes through."

The Production Manager said, "Yes."

Then, I asked, "Can we know the exact identification of these resources?"

The Production Manager fumbled.

I said, "The asset code!"

He understood and we assigned, G03, S02, F03 and P08 codes to the boxes that were connected sequentially by unidirectional arrows, from left to right.

Then I said "We need a sense of utilization of these machines. It doesn't need to be very accurate."

The managers looked blank.

I said, looking at Kunal, "In the morning, we saw utilization numbers, can we look back into them and figure out the gross utilization numbers for these resources?"

Kunal had worked out the utilization numbers based on some cost accounting principles and I knew that these numbers would vary over a wide range, but I did not wish to challenge their accuracy.

I said, "We do not need to be accurate here, but it is enough to see the relative utilization."

Soon we had the XL™ sheet of asset utilization and then I said, "How much for Gating Operations?"

Kunal said, "Sorry, we do not have a number there, because we use processors that have huge capacity than any other down steam process, hence we do not check its utilization, and it would be around 10%."

"Wonderful," I said. "We do not need its utilization."

"Shaping!"

"20%"

"Finishing!"

"40%"

"Packing!"

"55%"

I wrote down all these numbers into the process boxes that I had drawn on the white board.

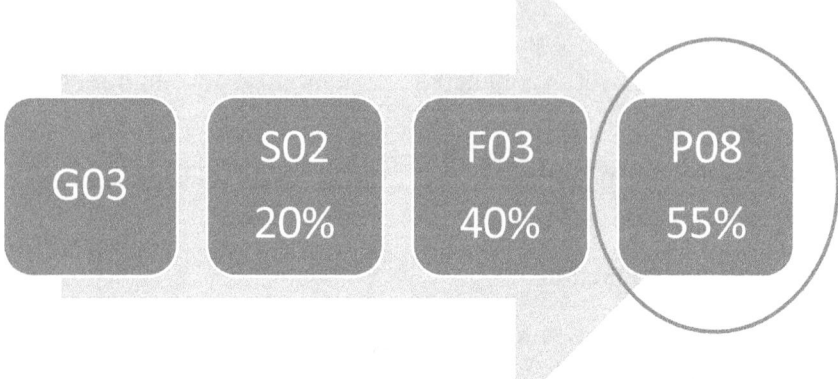

Figure 6.4 The process flow at the Plant and the likely constrained resource

And said, "So, it means that the utilization of Finishing and Packing along the path of the Leveraged Product is significantly higher compared to that in the Gating and Shaping areas. It means that we have less capacity left in these machines than those in Gating and Shaping. Hence, our scope of higher throughput is prevented by these or one of these machines. If we need to increase our throughput along this line, we must improve our productivity on Shaping or Packing machines."

Now since, the data on utilization was very gross and there could be an error of as much as 20%, it was not necessary to get into more accurate data, rather I asked one question. "On day to day basis, where do we have pressures running high, in Finishing or Packing…?"

The Production Manager said, "We are comfortable with Finishing, we have a lot of issues in packing. That is where we have too much overtime."

"Actually, Sir, 10 products pass through P08," said a colleague of the Production Manager.

"Interesting," then, I suggested that we take P08 as the machine for the next level of investigation.

I also said, "However, if we make any mistake i.e., the most utilized machine is not P08 but F02, we will correct ourselves quickly without losing much time and effort."

"No no! Packing is the bottle neck, I bet," said the Production Manager with great assertion.

"Very good! This only gives us more confidence to get into further investigation," I said.

Capturing the Leveraged Data Set

"Now can we do one thing? We need the log book of P08 quickly." I said.

"Log book...," said Anup Das.

I saw people staring at me, "Actually, we need more than one log book. We need log books for last 4 months."

The Production Manager sent his colleague to fetch the log books.

I added, "Now we need to do a very simple and dirty work."

People looked at me with awe.

I said "Yes a very dirty work, which you would hate to do, but believe me by tomorrow morning you would be so happy and proud of yourself that you did it."

Then, I revealed, "As we get the log books, we need to digitize them. We need to enter the content into XL™ sheets and this is to be done NOW. In essence, we would be entering product name, batch number, and their respective start and end timings for the packing operation, into the XL™ sheet. We are going to type them and then, do some analysis."

"I know that throughout our lives we have handled a lot of data. But this piece of data is extremely important and it has the clue for productivity improvement, which we must believe now.... I am extremely sorry to put you into this trouble, but however much we hate this, we must enter it immediately. You are going to enter the data written by your operators into your laptops, and this may be demeaning for your designation, but let's do it to know the power of right data. And believe me… there is huge money hidden in this data. If you ever said, data is money… time has come to validate it. Tomorrow, by 12 O'clock noon you would know that you have worked on the best data set you ever come across." I was serious about this piece of work.

Kunal said, "No problem Sir, we are going to be here to see that we complete this work today itself."

In the meanwhile, the log books arrived and I gave guidance on which part of the logbook to be entered. When I saw them struggling to begin typing, I took over their laptop and prepared a template. Made entry for one batch and then, asked Kunal's colleagues (Finance Managers) to follow through.

The data entry started…, there were a lot of inconsistencies in the data and for the first time they realized that people were entering data for the sake of entering; things were illegible, mistakeful, clumsy and overwritten. And somebody had said that the logbooks were important from regulatory point of view!

The twosome was busy typing in data from the log books. As the data started coming up on the screen and there were around 10 records already keyed in; the Production Manager, the Export Manager, the HR Managers and the CFO, were glued onto them and were trying to do some analysis. Their jaws were drooping and they were gossiping amongst themselves.

It was already 5:30 pm, and I was feeling weary, I knew that the data entry would take time.

I asked Kunal if I could leave, since doing the data entry might take some time.

Kunal talked to the managers and said them to spend their time 'as long as it takes' and complete it before they leave for home. He also asked them to postpone some other reports and transfer some work to him, but focus on digitization of the logbook data.

I requested them to send the file as soon as they would finish. And then, I said to the team, "Tomorrow, I am going to do a presentation at 9:00am on the findings."

I shook hands with them and left the room with Tapas, Manas and Kunal.

As Manas drove me and Kunal towards the Hotel; to them, the picture was becoming clearer. They had already seen something in the data points and thanked me for the process they went through.

At sharp 9:00pm, I got an SMS from the Chairman's secretary, "Sir Mail Sent, kindly check." As I deleted the SMS, two more SMS buzzed on my cell phone, one from the CFO and another from the Finance Manager ....confirming the mail.

I opened my mail box. Saw the XL™ sheet. The team had done extremely good work. They had looked into the data, identified the holidays, the non working days and cleaned up the data quite a bit from the outliers.

They also included additional columns that indicated the process time of each batch and the idle time between good batches.

As I snapped the first dataset into a graph; my eyes opened wide. The first graph was telling a big story and revealing an unbelievable scope of productivity improvement. I quickly made a few more graphs and plugged them into the power point presentation that I had already prepared after returning from the Plant.

I left conclusion of my slide blank and wanted to sleep over the day's proceeding. The exhaustion of the day was catching up with me and the cozy room at the Park Hotel was inviting me to relax. I went to the bed early.

Management Briefing

I got up early.

I ran through the presentation, did a bit of editing, looked into the graphs, made some back of the envelop estimates and wrote my comments.

Around 8:15am the Chairman, Jayant Sen and the Director, Tapas came to pick me up. On the way, I looked at Jayant Sen and said, "Yesterday, we made a lot of progress and everything went as we wanted. I must thank your team for taking the need of improvement positively. There were a lot of emotions in the room, but emotions are part of life and it only means that people care so much about the company. I must also thank your CFO and his team that they sat yesterday till late evening to do a very dirty work, which was to type the log book data of a packing machine."

"Yes, I came to know about it," said Jayant Sen.

I said, "I am sorry, I had to ask for that because this dataset contains the clue for our next big action."

Tapas said, "No no, this is very important work, and thank you for this. If needed all of us would have been there."

Then, I explained the approach we took to develop the methodology to quickly zero onto likely area of focus, after Jayant Sen had left the day before. They were excited.

I opened my lap top and explained the particular slides on the methodology. Once I showed them how we identified the weakest link for 10 products, Tapas was excited and said, "I find it very simple and intuitive. It dramatically reduces the complexity of thinking and gives a very high clarity for actions."

Then I showed them the graphs that came out of the analysis of logbook data. They were shocked to see the amount of variability and idle time. Their faces turned red, but Jayant Sen said, "I am not angry with this view, but really shocked to know that this is the situation at our most constrained machine. It tells us how big scope of opportunity we have, there must be reasons for these though."

I said, "Yes, since there is so much of variability, it may not be possible to right away identify the reasons, rather it would be good to accept this situation. We must realize that there is huge hidden capacity and start a process that will gradually reveal the hidden capacity."

He said, "Yes, we will do as you say."

On the way to the Plant, I gave them a dope on variability and how it dramatically impacts performance of any business. I gave them examples of several different businesses, on the type of variability and how they are grappling with it, how some are able to deal effectively and also the tools and methodology to deal with it. I wanted them to realize that *the organizational capability of dealing with the situation needed an upgrade and it needed to get onto a way of achieving it which could be done without taking too much risks and too much cost.*

The Show Time

It was around 9 O'clock by the time we entered the conference hall. Everybody got up and wished us. It had all chairs occupied except three, and I saw a few new faces. I wished everybody and shook hands. Then I introduced myself to the new faces.

When we entered the hall, the team was running through the logbook data and trying to make sense out of it. They were looking at average, mean, median, standard deviation etc. The CFO was busy on his calculator and was vigorously working out something.

After Jayant Sen and Tapas took their seats, I walked up to the CFO and told that I would make a presentation. I requested him to get me the projector cable and then, connected my laptop. It opened the first page of my presentation.

I said, "Good morning everybody! Yesterday, we had a good brain storming session. I hope that all of you liked it. The idea of yesterday's discussion was to bring all of us to the realization that we have a common problem and none of us is a problem. And we need to deal with this problem together. We also wanted to make us realize that variability of all sorts, unless prepared for, creates much of the performance degradation. We also discussed that recalling events after a long gap and trying to solve the problem is not in the best interest and will not help. And since, there are several events and problems that prevent us from increasing our throughput, it is not physically possible to better manage the business, however many people we add. What's needed is not to be reactive to events but have a methodology that allows us to build the required capability and improve the business, simultaneously. For which, *we need to embrace variability.* "

"Yesterday itself, after my visit to the plant, we started working on demonstrating a process that would give us an immediate benefit. And when I left in the evening, I said that by today, you would be extremely satisfied that we have a glimpse of the huge success in such a short time."

I then walked up to the CFO and his two managers, shook hands with them again and said to them, "What did we say yesterday, before we left you here with data entry."

The CFO said, "We are going to do a very dirty work. But by 12 O'clock today, we would realize that the dataset, on which we work, is the best dataset we ever worked in our life; because growth of the company is hidden in this limited set of data. And we would be proud of ourselves that we created it."

I said to Jayant Sen, "I would like to thank them for having faith in the new process that we are going to build."

Then I said, "Ok... so let's start."

"Based on what I learnt so far, the objective of the company is to provide goods which help its clients do better business."

"In order to do justice with its objective, the company must on an ongoing basis provide more and more quality goods to the market. It means that despite turbulent times, the company must achieve a sustainable growth."

We are here to find a way that will put the company on a sustainable growth path irrespective of the changes around. Is not it, a good way to start with." I asked.

"Yes, it is the right way," said Jayant Sen.

The first set of slides was about history and description of the company as I knew. It identified domestic and exports markets, and the respective revenues.

The next slide was on pressure points.

I said, "Currently, the company is waiting for its new plant to come up. However, it will take a while before this plant rolls out newer and high-end products into the developed markets. A huge amount of company's money is locked in this plant for over past two years. Which means that cash is definitely a constraint. Whether anybody accepts this or not, we must recognize the subsequent pressures it builds up directly or indirectly into rest of other operations."

"Correct!" I said while seeking their response.

"Absolutely," said the CFO and others nodded affirmatively.

Then, I said, "Domestic market is currently comfortable, although, competition is picking up here."

"Almost a decade back, a strategic call was taken to enter into white label market abroad and now there are over 200 products offered to this segment. This is a big opportunity. Exploiting such an opportunity is *Simple but not Easy*, as we understood yesterday. We must remember that we are not talking about two countries but about two big and complete continents, and hence, the challenges are multifold. Building a capability to meet these challenges is critical."

"And we know today, the profitability of the organization despite so many years of good performance is going down." Said Kunal.

"The margins for white labels are extremely low, it takes 80% of resources but gives only 20% of throughput and the delivery terms are highly non competitive against both smaller and larger competitors. But our future depends on growth of this segment." He emphasized.

I added, "Since these are MTO (Made to Order) channels, we do not have the benefit of aggregation of stock. More so because the volumes have not yet kicked in despite a large enough portfolio."

"The Long Tail there from, leads to large orders for just a few products but extremely different tiny orders for most of the products. This means a large number of changeovers in the plant. Which means lower utilization of resources, which means more number of people, which means more resources, which mean more complexity; so more people and so more cost."

"Right!" I said, as I walked towards the team.

"Yes," several people said in unison.

"So we know why our costs might seem to be high if they are high. I am currently not saying that costs are high."

"And we have over thirty different problems in fulfilling requirements of export market. We have fallen into a sort of vicious cycle and are not able to come out of this seemingly complex situation."

Leveraging Past Decisions and Experience

"Now castigating the export market so much, does not mean that the decisions that led to the Long Tail phenomenon was wrong. It was absolutely right when the decision was taken to go for exports market, offer more products and postpone profitability. The idea at that time was to build a base, build experience and understand the market. But the situations at that time and this time are different. Several parameters of environment outside and inside have changed. Now, we need to review our assumptions and make the right level of correction. This will further include making certain new assumptions, which we must give sometime to stabilize."

"How is our comfort level with the knowledge of the market now?" I asked while looking at Manas.

"The good thing is that we have far more knowledge of the export market. We know from our experience which of rules work and which not. Which products run fast and which not. Which customers are reliable and which not. Which geography has future potential and which not. We know the working of the market. We know the cause and effect in the market with a confidence level that is far more than the one we had started a decade back with."

Then, I said, "The biggest thing that we have today is 'our willingness to review our decisions of past and be ready to reverse operational decisions if they need be'. Nothing is bigger than this, and this is a specialty of this organization, and we need this unique culture to be in our value system."

"Certainly, now the time has come to leverage the past experience and our value system." said Jayant Sen.

Business Fundamentals

I said, "Yesterday, we discussed about business fundamentals. And we said that a business is created to earn money and not save money. This means that we must start by asking ourselves to find a way to increase revenue first, and in doing so we must be cost effective. In fact, a serious effort in increasing revenue will also reduce the relative cost. Generally, we must try to avoid a separate initiative to reduce cost unless there are glaring costly elements."

"I think that we need to review our cost reduction projects and align them with revenue potential," said Tapas and made a note in his diary.

Market Focus

I continued, "And then, we said that we must start working backward from the market and see what prevents us in our backend from getting more revenue from the market. We realized that the variability (the Long Tail seemingly being the biggest) created by the market must be dealt with. And we took a decision to review the tail and rationalize it. I must repeat here that we can't eliminate the Long Tail for it is an inherent characteristics of this industry.

What we recognize is that this Long Tail got built up as a natural process of market experimentation. However, the backend capability did not grow sufficiently to deal with the variability produced by the longer than the Long Tail. Probably, once we build this capability we would be able to handle such a long tail. Rationalizing the long tail now will give us a breathing time to catch up with our capability and improve our current performance in this market."

Manas got up, walked up to me and gave me a sheet of paper. It showed the initial list of products that the team intended to choke and those it expected an improved demand from.

"Thank you. Good work." I said, as I looked at the list that came earlier than I expected.

Focused Approach to Identify Leverage Point inside the Plant

Then, I said, "The way to demonstrate quickly that we can have quick improvement is to first build effectiveness and then efficiency.   There is a word used in Finance called "leverage point". A leverage point (Pivot) offers a significantly higher level of effectiveness and an order of magnitude increase in output for a relatively tiny effort. We now need a pivotal approach to improve things in our backend."

Kunal nodded in affirmation.

One of the best ways to identify Pivot in the plant is to pick a product from the market such that if we do any improvement in the back end (the Plant), we can see immediate additional revenue from this product. Hence, yesterday in the afternoon, we worked out to find a product that Manas said will be sold immediately even if we produce double the quantity."

"Actually, the discussion of yesterday, led us to identify criteria to select leveraged products and build a process to identify Leverage Point inside the plant." I went to the next slide, as I said.

"I need to emphasize here that we had a brief discussion on this. We must have a fairly standardized and separate process built for selection of leveraged products, since yesterday's process was a rough process just because we had less time." I then asked the CFO to enter it in the minutes of the meeting. But I cautioned, "There can't be too many criteria."

The next slide showed the list of six products which together made 70% of the sales. And, one product was marked with red circle. I said, "This product marked with red circle is chosen as the Leveraged Product."

This led to discussion on why this product and not the other. The discussion settled down quickly, when I mentioned that it did not matter which product as long as we were able to demonstrate the process of improvement, and the other products would fall into the process soon.

Tapas said, "Yes, I understood that we are trying to come out with a process, so it is ok with this product."

The Leverage Point Decides the Capacity to Make Money

The next slide showed the process flow of the product, and the constrained operation P08 was encircled in red.

Then, I said, "P08 decides how much can be produced from this Leveraged Product. If we increase utilization numbers here, we will get more revenue. Is this clear?"

I gave time, and then asked again, "Is it right that one extra hour on this machine per day will give extra revenue?"

"Yes," "Of course!" people said, though at first they tried to assimilate the question.

"One extra hour per day means 30 extra hours a month, means almost two extra days of work...Now you know the benefit. And possibly, the benefit directly goes to the bottom line without an extra penny added to operating expenses."

"Oh! Yeah!" exclaimed Tapas.

"And in most of such cases, it will be more than one extra hour." I pushed for bigger opportunity.

Then, they started discussing and questioning the utilization numbers of the resources shown in the slide. The CFO intervened and said, "This is a gross utilization, and is not so accurate, but good enough for taking decision required for moving to the next step. It is in the range of +/-20%, we do not need to go into its details right now." I thanked him.

I went to the next slide. It showed all other products that passed through the Constrained Resource. They were precisely 10. Then I said, "We understand that if the utilization of this resource is increased by 10%, we would get 10% more output. Which means that an improvement of 10% utilization of this resource (P08) will increase throughput of all the 10 products by 10%."

"Wonderful," said Jayant Sen, he grasped things quickly.

"What does it mean?" I asked

Anup Das said, "*We started with the Leveraged Product, went back into the Plant, traced one resource that limits its throughput, and now if we increase utilization of this resource, it is going to increase performance of 10 products not just one.* Wonderful, a very good logical connection!"

"Yes, this is the power of focused approach," said Kunal, the CFO.

The next slide showed exactly what the Plant Manager had said. It showed the focusing approach that led from company level problems through market through plant to the one resource that held the Lever for improving performance of 10 products at one go.

It was an impressive way of describing the approach and I titled the slide "Problem Identification- Quick and Effective Approach."

After that, I again looked at Jayant Sen and thanked the CFO team for the data they gathered on the Pivot machine (Leverage Point). I then provided metadata on the investigation on P08, including the products and number of batches produced during the past 120 days.

The Information that Broke Hearts

Then..., I said, "Here it is," and displayed the slide containing the process time of the machine, P08.

A graph was shown for the batches of one dominant product that passed through P08 during the past 4 months. I said, "The X-axis shows the chronologically produced batches of one product and the Y-axis shows the time it is loaded on the machine."

I continued, "Look at the peaks and valleys, which says that this product which we say as the key product and which is a stable product, has a process time that varies over 300%." The process time was varying wildly over 300%, without any pattern and bounds, revealing a highly uncontrolled process.

It took some time for the team to understand the definition of process time, the graph and then.... There was huge commotion and loud discussions.

People could not believe it. The Production Manager who had championed so much on his kaizen and standardization of work practices, now started blaming raw materials, change in priority, people's unavailability etc.

Rest of the people wanted to see more granular data. The relevant worksheets of the XL™ file were displayed. Disbelieving the numbers there, people wanted to verify it with the log books.

The log books were brought back into the hall. Each column on the XL™ sheet was explained, as if people did not know what a log sheet was, and it was tallied with the logbook entries. I was really embarrassed in maintaining my patience while explaining their own document to them.

Instead of making valuable managerial sense out of the slide, people started cursing the slide and were looking deeper into each hour and minute in the log book. It opened up a big brawl. Each batch that could be recognized was being identified and justification was asked for the deviation from some vague standard time. In fact, the organization had no single standard process time of the batch. The Production Manager was getting cornered; and every time he had no answer, he would say "Sir, this decision was taken in Director's meeting ...."

I had to intervene, "As I said earlier, we are unfortunately getting into details that are not necessary in this forum. In any case, trying to recall reason for delay of a batch that was processed weeks before, has no meaning, nobody will remember. We need to stop trying to react to events. And take the key observations from the graph, to help us in putting a managerial process that will improve the situation. Let us not get bogged down into data... there would be more than 30 reasons why delays occur and it makes no sense to talk about them sitting in this room."

Barely did I reinforce my advice, Tapas looked at the HR manager, and said, "When every day I check with you, I am told that your people are going around the plant and machines are started at 8:00am. Look at the data, no batch is started before 10:00am. What type of feedback mechanism do you have? Are your people going there? Are they sending right messages to you?"

"I will look into it, Sir." The HR Manager was cryptic.

Tapas was not happy, and said, "This is not a production problem; this is a simple HR problem and a simple matter of discipline. Please ensure that from tomorrow, we have machines started in time."

Jayant Sen said, "I think that from tomorrow we need to capture reasons of delays for all such machines. Please prepare a template and let me have a look at it."

The Production Manager said, "Yes, we will do."

Tapas was in no mood to stop and a whole lot of brawl started again; and I had tough time in calming down the team.

Once the team calmed down, the next slide was the time diagram of P08 specifically for the Leveraged Product and that too showed a huge variability in process time. People wanted to see further details but I said that it made no sense to get into details, as the issue was already discussed in the previous slide.

I said, "The message is that there is a huge variability in the time it takes to process the same SKU on machine P08, and it is in the range of 100-300%, irrespective of the product and packing size. So we recognize this variability. We do not have to answer it now, and it makes no sense to try to recall the reasons for variability. The next step is to draw a generally acceptable process time for the respective products and then from tomorrow start monitoring and noting down reasons for the delay of each and every batch. Then, the reasons for delay must be systematically analyzed. And Anup's team has knowledge of all the tools required to improve productivity of P08."

"The secret, once we get this monitoring mechanism in place, is the analysis of the reasons using Pareto chart and having an effective system in place to deal with them. However, on day to day basis, we need to act on the upcoming delays quickly. For which we need a mechanism of escalation. People are good and want to solve problems themselves, however, in a supply chain and in an organization, problems can not be allowed to stay with single person for longer time and they must be escalated as fast as possible. Issues must be brought up to the notice of seniors before it is too late and expediting must be avoided."

The team had a lot of confusion about escalation and expediting. Tapas said, "A significant part of the problems that we see, occurs because we escalate when it needs to be expedited, and expedite when it needs to be escalated."

The team then asked me if I had a process of escalation. I said, "I have one, I would show a document but I request you to prepare your own, since the specifics will vary from organization to organization based on the culture and individual capability. A more matured organization will have shorter escalation time and very few expediting events."

The Much Awaited Hidden Capacity

As the team seemed to settle down, I said, "Let's move ahead, but I request you to not get into more fact finding and assigning reasons NOW. Let's try to take managerial output from the data set. Please do not get into issues of shop floor level in this room."

I clicked onto the next slide. It was displaying the changeover time for all the batches produced on the leveraged machine during the last 120 days. I again explained them the X and Y axis. And with caution, I read the comments that were annotated there.

I did not allow any body to speak or any gossip to occur. I said, "The average changeover time per batch is 9 hours."

I went to the white board and circled a number that was written earlier '2.5 to 3 hrs', a precise range of change over time that the Production Manger had quoted, during the earlier discussion.

I said, "Look at the perception we have and the reality. We are off from standard time by a huge margin."

"How can it be…,"said the Production Manager.

"Have we taken out the holidays and voluntary breaks from our calculations?" asked the HR Manager.

Hesitatingly, I flashed the XL™ sheet, where each holiday including the weekends and each voluntary break, was clearly marked in red and accounted for. The HR Manager walked up to the projected image to check if it was accounted for.

Not able to accept the reality, the Production Manger said as he looked at the Finance Manager, "We operate only 2 shifts a day, did you take that the break into account."

His desperation was simmering up. Tapas was staring at him, while shaking his head in disbelief.

They again cross checked… and it was indeed accounted for.

The Finance Managers had done the hard work to normalize, cleanup and harmonize the data, for they knew that this type of 'data validation' related questions would pop up first. I thanked them for taking care of the nuances.

Then, I said, "Please understand once again, we are not talking about high accuracy of data, there may be some error. Let me admit, there would be some error, but it is ok. What we need to see is the amount of deviation between the reality and our perception; and even if you make a huge discount on account of data integrity, we will still have huge gap in performance. And *it is sufficient to recognize that what we perceive is not what the reality is. And, the difference is huge*."

Everybody was working on numbers, and curious gossiping had started. Jayant Sen and Tapas too started talking to each other since I had stopped them from raising their voice.

The CFO called me, showed his calculator and spoke into my ears, "Our production for these products could be more than doubled; *in any case we can get at least 20% additional capacity in no time*. This is huge."

I said, "Keep calm, we need to take one step at a time."

The Take Away

I pulled attention of people again. "So here is what we need to take from this slide and from the other slides we saw so far. There is a huge opportunity to improve throughput. And now if we workout, we would not only be able to give Manas extra volumes for the leverage products, probably for all the products. How do you feel Manas?" I asked him.

He said, "Excellent, it can never be better than this. I am overwhelmed with our findings."

And then I said, "Now we know that there is a significant hidden capacity and that there is a simpler way to identify the weak links (the Leverage Point), we must now start working on the implementation. Please remember that an hour lost on the Leverage Point (P08) is an hour lost for the complete line, and an hour gained on the Leverage Point is an hour gained for the

151

complete line. And if our current utilization of P08 is at 30%, an extra hour per day mean 2 extra days of process time, which is around 20% increase in throughput. *Unless any other resource on the line becomes constrained, looking at the variability in process time and the amount of idle time, we must get much more hidden capacity out."*

"There should not be any difficulty, what so ever, in getting 20% more throughput from P08," said Tapas in a commanding voice.

"Since, the leverage product comprises just 10% of the volume processed on P08, if the revealed 20% capacity is allocated to it, we can produce more than double the number of batches," Manas pushed his intentions.

"Yes, it should more than take care of what we promised you yesterday, Manas," said Anup Das.

"When it comes to implementation, please understand that the solution to each problem (identified reason for delays), will come from shop floor and not from this room. And please do not make the mistake of suggesting solution from this room. Put a monitoring mechanism and a review system that allows people to see the 'weakest link' (Leverage Point) and the sharply identified opportunities to improve. The only decision need to be taken in this meeting is about starting of monitoring and carrying out improvement on the machine (the Leverage Point)."

I also cautioned, "I would request to allow the production team to start its work and rest of us must wait at least a week for the new practice to stabilize."

Most important thing, "Do not jump to all the products and all machines trying to monitor everything. First work on P08 and go through the complete cycle of improvement that must be without taking any risk and without costing additional penny."

The next slide summarized two actions

    1. Rationalize long tail
    2. Start monitoring on P08

Then I said, "Please understand that this is just the beginning, we are yet to talk about achieving On Time Delivery. This issue, we would take up later on."

"I feel that the capacity that we would surface at P08 will automatically improve our cycle time and On Time Delivery as well," said Manas.

"May be yes, but there are more fundamental elements we need to address before we achieving high On Time Delivery. We will look at it later on." I said.

Final Words- The Beginning
And then I gave my concluding remark.

"The company has made great progress during last 40 years. However, the business environment continues to be more and more unpredictable. There are an increasing number of variables that is impacting the business. The recent dip in performance despite of several new initiatives is an indication that the team needs to upgrade its capability to deal with the variability in the environment. We must develop a capability to deal with apparently complex situation *without shaking up the complete organization*. I look forward to the implementation of the methodology we have identified since yesterday and the validation that it works.

What we have seen and achieved thus far, is just the beginning and would affect only small fortune of the business. We must recognize that the business comprises a number of interdependent building blocks. As we start working in one area, it will impact other areas and will put pressure points to make further improvements. We must now set out our mind to this process of identifying Leverage Points and releasing capacity. The actions that we are going to take from tomorrow, will affect, sales, marketing, HR, Quality, R&D and even the domestic market for all of them are interconnected. And to deal with all these effects, we need to build superior capability of ongoing improvement. Let's then build this process further.

I request that we consider the identified machine P08, as the Pivot and do all our experiments of improvements here, before we jump onto other areas.

And do remember, people are good. There is nothing wrong with them. Something else is creating lower performance, more delays and higher cost. We need to address the root cause. And once you start exploiting P08, you would realize that even machines may not be the constraints. The real constraint would be various policies that are framed by us sitting in this room that prevent the company from moving to the next desired level. We must be humble and ready to work on them as soon as they are identified."

The story went on... as the team at Infaproducts committed itself to puts back the organization on sustainable growth path...on a path of operational excellence....

....

What did the team do after identifying the Leverage Point, how much capacity it could reveal, what obstacles came up on its way in dealing with the constraints, which new techniques and tools did it adopt to release the capacity and what was the overall impact of its actions on the business results?

Answers to these and many more questions are captured in a 260 page game changing business novel 'The Path - Leveraging Operations in a Complex and Chaotic World'.

If your organization is under tremendous pressure to increase capacity and you are planning to invest your time, money and effort in huge CAPEX budget, check the possibility of revealing hidden capacity in your plants. In case you need guidance in identifying and revealing hidden capacity in your plants, call the Author and take the Capacity Hunt Challenge with him.

Capacity Hunt Challenge will be conducted by the Author with your team. In less than 30 hours your team will be able to identify the hidden capacity and will be ready to march on the path of realizing benefits of revealing hidden capacity, without taking real risk and without causing costly trade-offs.

What is the Rule of Thumb for Stock Levels?

It is not by Calculations but by the Process

May3rd 2012

Last quarter, one of my clients built a natural process of inventory control and recently, they described it in the form of guidelines. Subsequently, I found several requests including a discussion in a LinkedIn group for a rule of thumb for stocking levels.

Well we know that things change with time and static rule of thumb may not serve the purpose. You need a process that allows an acceptable level of inventory. Most often the decision is not how much inventory is needed, rather it is about how do I have a process that addresses the dilemma of sometime having too less stock (stock out) and other time having too high stocks (expiries, non-moving stocks, returns, money locked).

Here is a sample description and question I am often asked to answer.

…start…

I have 30 days of committed orders and above it, we forecast for 60 days. Hence, we have orders for 90 days (a quarter of the year) in our operational horizon. With time, orders add into 'committed orders', which may be from the 'forecasted ones' or 'new orders of different products or specifications'. The committed orders in fact, could change almost in the range of -5% to 25% over a 30 day load on day to day basis. Of course, once in a quarter we may have spiked orders of more than 10 days work.

We do use some sort of forecasting, but you know it is never accurate for operations and it never works, rather creates a lot of mismatches and tension. Forecast does seem useful though, for advanced planning and preparation with suppliers and sometime for capacity management. We do have intuition that for effective operations, we need something at the level of scheduling and stock management than long term based planning.

Under above situation, we often run out of stocks for several products and we get brickbats from our customers as well as from our sales team for not honoring the promise of due date or ready availability of certain products. On the other hand, at any time, a substantial number of our products are overstocked and lie in our FG stores for too long a time, which locks my money and invites ire of my CEO and CFO.

In every meeting I am hammered to ensure availability on one hand, while I am warned of bad consequences on my next promotions if I do not keep my inventory down to 30 days. My inventory level fluctuates in the range of 75 days to 90 days.

Well this is only half the story, I have to take care of raw materials as well, whose variety is no fewer than that of our saleable products (SKUs).

I feel that 30 days inventory is not realistic, while my bosses feel that anything above 30 days is a professional crime. What do I do?

…end…

Direction for solving the Dilemma
Input Data Set:

Orders in Hand: 30 days, Forecast: +60 days over Orders in Hand

Demand variability: -5%+25%, Spiked Demand: up to 50%

Number of Raw Materials: 300 Expected inventory = 30 days

Current inventory levels = 75-90 days

Assumptions:

> 1. Inventory under discussion is finished goods inventory (200 items)
> 2. FG Inventory is in the plant before dispatch

Basics

There are some rules for the shop-floor:

1. Inventory in hand (FG inventory) is not decided, rather it is maintained. We need to allow the internal operational processes and demand dynamics to suggest what would be the 'Inventory in hand.'

2. Pipeline inventory for a class of product is equal to maximum consumption during a reliable replenishment time. Where, Pipeline inventory comprises items in the stock and those in progress (WIP). However, effort can always be made to reduce the inventory drastically without jeopardizing availability.

RM Stock   WIP in shop floor   FG Stock

Figure 6.5 Inventory in the Production Pipeline.

Further, having a stock level that provides enough safety for the replenishment time and a factor of safety is good enough. However, it is very difficult to get an 'exact' replenishment time.

Explanation

It is not whether you should have 30 days stock-in-hand or 60 days stock-in-hand. You need to have enough inventories so that you do not stock out when there is a customer order. At the same time you don't stock so much that your money is stuck in inventory (and the system response slows down).

The guiding factor therefore, is to have just enough inventory, which is proportional to the consumption pattern during a replenishment time.

More explanation…

Normally average demand and average replenishment time are used for estimating inventory. But an 'average' is an 'average'. In day to day operations, peaks and troughs occur leading to bullwhip effect (excess of load in one place and starvation in other places). Thus, 'average' number invariably leads to underestimation and overestimation. Right inventory never works and we get into a vicious cycle that impinges upon us in the form of dilemma as described above.

Average is a good way of treating the available data and starting estimation of inventory (unless your forecasting in reasonably accurate, not only in terms of how much but also in which sequence products be consumed by the market).

So, if we do not have a high confidence in forecasting and averaging is the only other way of handling demand, then we start with average but establish a process that corrects the under and over estimation before the dilemma hits us. Here is a practical way. But before that some more basic understanding…

More Basics

Inventory in hand is a derivative of what is called Pipe Line inventory (for the Production).

 Pipeline inventory = FG inventory + WIP inventory

The Pipeline inventory is estimated as the maximum demand over a period of reliable replenishment time. And a rule for shop floor operations is:

Pipeline inventory levels = (Average Demand x Demand variability factor) x (Average Replenishment time x operational reliability factor)

While you can get the average numbers, based on past as well as future, common sense tells us that variability factor is something which we need to arrive at by gazing and monitoring the variation. We need to establish it empirically. It will vary from industry to industry, organization to organization and plant to plant based on the product portfolio and operational maturity. Never the less, there is no need to worry about its accuracy, start with something that is not ridiculously on extremes. And then the rule of operations is to *allow the system to correct the error.* How?

Here it is.

The Process

Objective: To establish a simple and intuitive inventory 'control' system that keeps inventory at just enough levels that do not cause extreme levels of stock-out and non-movables.

1. Set initial pipeline inventory by using replenishment time, consumption rate and a variability factor. The outcome need not be very accurate (believe in the saying from economics: *it is better to be roughly right than precisely wrong.*)

2. Install a procedure to monitor stock-in-hand for key products where you have concerns (a quick review of your stocks will tell you that you need not monitor 100% of your product portfolio). This is good because you any way do not have all the time in world to do only monitoring.

3. Whether you like it or not, with time, stocks of some products would move towards the bottom while those of others will languish near or above the top. Consider, your observations during a reasonable period and then:

    1. If stocks in hand for certain products 'chronically' hit the bottom, increase the pipeline stock levels by a predetermined level. This will also mean releasing additional orders. The assumption is that you have enough capacity in the plant, otherwise focus on improving performance of your bottleneck.
    2. If stocks in hand for certain products 'chronically' stay at the top, decrease the pipeline stock levels by a predetermined level. This means that you may also need to stop releasing some of the process orders of these products.

What should be the interval of review and the level of increase or decrease of inventory? It depends on the level of risk you associate to 'stock out' and 'overstock'. Normally, review once per replenishment time is good enough. For some organizations, 'stock out' would be riskier than 'overstock', while it could be the other way for other organizations.

This is how you correct your inventory levels on an ongoing basis. Trying to be accurate here does not work, and you would unnecessary be playing into the noise and stressed up in the dilemma of stock control.

Of course, when you have seasonality and unprecedented spikes in demand and your level of confirmed orders goes well beyond 30 days, then you will need a well planned intervention not only into controlling the Pipeline stock but also in scheduling the complete operations.

Where is My Thumb Rule?

Now if that is so much about the Pipeline stock, then what about the thumb rules for stock-in-hand? Yes, ideally it should be around 50% of the pipeline inventory. So you have 50% stock-in-hand and 50% in WIP. *Whether the stock in hand should be of 30 days or 45 days, it depends on your replenishment time.*

So if your boss says reduce the inventory to 30 days. Check what is replenishment time after applying a factor of process variability? If for a product, it is less than 30 days, then you know that there is scope for reducing stock-in-hand. But if the replenishment is way beyond 30 days (in the example 75-90 days), you need to have discussion with your boss, because it may not be in your hand to reduce the stock levels. Remember that you are an inventory controller and not operations manager. You need to then bring in Operations team and crack the puzzle of long replenishment time. Yes... the indication is towards possible improvements in operations... and you know there is a journey called Operational Excellence.

A Departing Note

When you monitor stocks on regular basis, you could also use the relative status of stocks in hand for different products to set a priority system that gives you a non-complex scheduling system. It will give a significant jump in achieving high availability of products at lower stocks in hand. And also, you need to address the raw material issue too...

Retrieving Projects from Bad Performance

A Step Towards Easing the Gridlock at the Development Center

2nd Jul 2010

Projects are expected to be adventurous, successful completion of which not only gives tremendous fulfillment to its team but also provides significant return on investment to its sponsors. However, for teams of over 70% of the projects, working on projects is a frustrating experience that throws their normal life out of balance… and the dream of accomplishing an adventurous journey turns into mirage. They run into day to day conflicts that lie in the lack of understanding the very nature of the 'project' business and in the way they work. While projects are 'probabilistic' in nature, a vast majority of organizations tend to apply 'deterministic' rules in planning as well as in execution.

The below impromptu description brings out the fundamental nature of project and thereby, exhorts to follow rules favorable in achieving success in 'projects'. The difference between organizations that respect these rules and those who do not, is huge (e.g. due date performance of over 90% versus less than 40%).

…Start…

Two weeks back, I got a call from Anthony. He was chosen to start an initiative PROP-UP, to improve the overall project management performance of his center. This initiative came as a result of review of his development center last quarter. Significant gaps were found in the effectiveness of the management in delivering projects during past couple of years.

Anthony was working for my group five years back, when I had left the center to work my own venture. Things changed a lot since then. The number of scientists increased from 80 to 800, the count of open projects increased from 15 odd to over 200 and responsibility for managing several products worldwide increased manifold. This center was a global development center for a fortune 100 engineering giant. When I had left, a systematic project management practice had just begun and preparations were on for seeking advanced project management system certification.

This center was quite different compared to the regular engineering and development companies in India, in a way that it had a high percentage of people, who came from industrial system background and they had a high perspective of customers. Further, product development was a significant part of its activities.

Larger number of projects and people meant that it was a space of multi-projects, that had its own complications. Already, symptoms of sluggish execution had started hinting the management to search for areas of improvements. Anthony came to know from others about my involvement in TOC (theory of constraint), its application CCPM (critical chain project management) and how I was helping organizations in dramatically improving performance of their projects. He wanted me to have a look at issues faced by his center and help them moving in the right direction.

I therefore visited the center to *listen* to Anthony.

Anthony emphasized that his team was working on an initiative that came from the top management in Europe and it had total buy in from the center's Head. He said that a corporate announcement had already been made about PROP-UP and most importantly, a team of 4 senior managers was formed to spear head the initiative.

I was conscious that this was a big initiative and therefore, there was probably, a huge expectation from the management. An initiative that is big meant bigger goal and by nature, would mean bigger change, not only in processes and tools but also in the behavior of people. Bigger the change (bigger the goal)… means bigger the resistance to change. I, therefore, cautioned Anthony, to go one step at a time in a measured way. It was very important that for such a long journey, he gets wins as early as possible so that it would be possible to win support and create momentum... otherwise, mobilizing 800 people behind this change would be a herculean task.

My first question was, therefore, what the problem was and how big it was.

I did not get appropriate answer to this. 'Project performance is not satisfactory', was not the right answer to my question. I therefore told Anthony that he needed to set clear objective and metrics that could be a direct indicator of improvement through PROP-UP. It would then make sense for everybody to effect the right inputs and evaluate performance of their efforts.

His colleagues told me that the center had two goals, 1. Obtain good Due Date Performance (DDP) of the project and 2. Reduce Cost of the Center. This looked quite weird to me.

The reason being that firstly, an organization must have only one goal. Having two goals means confusion and conflicts galore, leading to misalignment down the rank. Secondly, the two goals were not mutually exclusively. That is, cost is a dependent on DDP and hence, if DDP is kept under control, cost would automatically come under control. Thirdly, 'cost' is normally not goal of an organization (even if it is a cost center) and is normally, not given as 'performance target' to managers. Why? Because, cost is a parameter, if taken as a target, managers start chasing it relentlessly and their efforts more often become detrimental to main purpose of the organization. And I believed that the purpose of an organization is not 'cost reduction'. Most importantly, *focus* on cost reduction would invariably lead to poor DDP.

Since, the center dealt in projects, it could be called a project based organization. Each project had a definite scope to be delivered within a cost and time frame. The truth was that a number of projects were abandoned midway and a large number of projects were late by huge margins compared to their first promised deadlines.

At the first moment of panic, the normal tendency in a project based organization is to cut down scope of the projects, in order to deliver them on time. These projects could be related to construction, engineering products, software development, infrastructure development, drug discovery etc. Project managers are worried too much on cost of the project and are involved in intense haggling with the sponsors about extra fee, whenever duration of projects need to be extended. Thus, projects are actually dominated by scope and cost factors. When these two factors are somehow adjusted, the negotiation hinges on the delivery dates. In a majority of the projects, despite all good intentions and compromises on scope and cost, the due date is extended too far, for the reasons that are *seemingly* not in the hands of either party. Thus, when the project is delivered, the project team looks at the *last agreed* due date of the project and comes out with a performance outcome that looks like following on its metrics:

Table 6.1 Typical Performance Metrics and What it Actually Means

Metrics	Delivered	What it actually means?
Scope	100%	Scope as readjusted and agreed (a few weeks before project was delivered), and in most cases it significantly deviates from originally agreed one.
Cost	100%	The extra cost compared to originally estimated one was readily borne by the client.
Time	DDP=97%	97% within the 'last agreed' date with the client. In most of the cases, the last agreed data is over 50% off the first agreed date.

In fact, when I asked Anthony and his team, about the DDP, they said above 97%. A few months back I had got the same answer, when I went on a call to meet the engineering team of a German Automotive component company. Then, I had asked them their definition of DDP. And it turned out that their definition of DDP as the performance of the project is 'delivery date' as compared to the 'last agreed date' and *not 'the first agreed' date*. A nice way to put the last delivery date is, 'mutually' agreed delivery date.

I insisted that they should let me know the performance with respect to the first agreed delivery date. His colleagues then said, "But this is how everybody measures project performance".

My answer was, "Of course, their results are also the same. Clients are not happy and everybody feels lost."

The issue then is "So if the DDP is 97%, then what are you complaining about? Is not this an extremely good performance? You and your customer must be very happy. But you also say that your customers are not very happy. And that they are becoming unhappier day by day. *It can't happen that your measurement shows one thing (that makes you happy) and your customers say the other (your customers are unhappy)*. May be that you need to see the way you measure your success; which is not same as the way customers measure their success and would like to measure your success. It thus means that your current measurements are not aligned with those of the customers."

It was very evident that the development center needed to correct its measurements and see where it was on that today. Then, it needed to set an achievable target and initiate improvements that would lift its performance and take it closer to its goal. Without correcting the measurement, having a performance level at 97% on a wrong scale would not allow the organization to target significant improvement. The idea was that performance would improve, if they knew the right parameter to measure and the inputs that directly influence this parameter.

The question then was in identifying what prevented the center from achieving a high DDP (from the *first committed due date*). Knowing what prevented, would shed light on possible ways of achieving improvement in performance.

At the center, people were measured on DDP not only of the project, but *also of the individual tasks*. Project managers spent 100s of hours in reviewing each project and each tasks day in day out. They were often *over paranoid* about the uncertainties and worked *much* beyond 8 hour schedule, *with an intention to get into details on smallest of activities*. They had the belief that if every task was brought under control the project would be under control. This was also the way they wanted to feel being hands-on and in control. Despite this, most of the projects missed deadlines by wide margins.

People are good, and they spend more than scheduled time without complaining, but it is not often a pleasant experience to complete a project. People overstretch themselves, imbalance their work and family life, and yet, get frustrated working on projects. There is no doubt about the intelligence, talent and domain knowledge levels of people. The center had a reputation of a sort of hiring people with unquestionable technical background; in the language of their competitors, its resource talent was awesome.

The Management too had good intention.

If the DDP (from first committed due date) of the project was poor despite everybody's best effort, the problem could be found on one or both of the following:

1. The assumptions (including estimations) made by the team were wrong
2. The way the tasks were implemented was not right.

It therefore, led me to probe into these two aspects. But wait a moment!

Are not we talking about a generic problem that is there in all project organizations? (e.g. the German Automotive Embedded System R&D Center, the Big Pharma's Innovation Center... and of course, India's leading software product development company. Not to forget the anemic conditions a majority of startup service companies fall into due to over 100% delays in their projects).

Yes, we are talking about generic problems that inflict project based organizations. And there are organizations who have come out of these problems. And their DDP (w.r.t. the first committed due date) is well above 95%.

Anthony's colleague had asked, "But organizations are different.... How can we apply the same thing here...?"

Well let's understand the following:

Problems are of two types, which could prevent the organization (whether it is a profit center or a cost center) from achieving its goal. Stating differently, there are two ways an organization can improve its performance.

1. By providing technical solutions
2. By improving logistical issues

What does it mean in the context of a development center? There are technical problems that are linked to material, machines, analysis, software knowledge, code, testing, hardware, energy, data bases, servers, drives etc. These problems can be solved by technical knowledge, research and actions; and there would be success, failures, slippages and breakdowns that are of technical nature.

But since, we are talking about a live organization that is already existing as a system, it has different teams, functions, departments, domains, specialization and tools; it has its own 'logistical' issues. While you create a product or a code, move it between people and deliver to client, it has to wait for decision and actions, it needs to be planned and scheduled, it needs to be verified and approved.... sequenced and timed....and managed. *In order for the already available technical contribution of its experts to make a business contribution, the center must pass the 'created value' through 'logistical channel' efficiently and effectively.*

Recent studies by leading researchers reveal that 'things are more complex than ever', 'employees know much more than they can deliver' and 'organizations expect their people to deliver to the level of their knowledge'. What it means is that we actually 'do' much much less than what we 'know'. This is clearly a management problem! The better the organization provides management tools, the better will be the delivery from their talented staff. A majority of the problems faced by project organizations is of this nature i.e. logistical.

While technical problems are quite different between domains, logistical problems have a large similarity, are systemic in nature and are traditionally referred as 'disruptions to flow'. Hence, these 'disruptions to flow of projects' that appear in one domain often reflect in others and, it is possible to adopt routine as well as innovative solutions from one domain into others.

FLOW of projects is something that managers need to be increasingly aware of, as complexity of their organization grows. Ultimately, it is the rate at which projects flow determines a project organization's performance NOW as well as in FUTURE.

The bottom line is that considering scientific competency of the Center at a significant maturity level, there could be a large possibility that project management competency from FLOW point of view, needs to be upgraded. It is like having good vehicles and good roads, but not so good way of managing traffic. It makes sense to invent a better way to regulate the flow than replacing all the vehicles and making huge investment in road infrastructure.

...

But we are still talking about poor performance of the organization in terms of DDP. It, therefore, behooves on the organization to have a clear perspective of 'project environment' before it identifies what to improve.

Worldwide, projects are given due dates and people are asked to stick to project due date as well as *task dues dates*. Projects are planned and people are given targets in a 'deterministic' way. Despite the fact that *project environment is 'probabilistic' in nature* (and not deterministic).

Anthony's teams kept screaming about the uncertainty they had in all projects, saying that their projects were different and that they had no way to meet the dates. And they knew that they could not claim to meet the due dates even before they would start execution.

They claimed that all the planning process is farce, since they did not know which logistical unknowns (and sometime technical unknowns) would suddenly crop up.

There were of course, risks, uncertainties, unknowns and unknowables. Bugs would be found late, just when they start a new task some other tasks would pop up on priority and plenty of rework keep disrupting the flow. When they plan a meeting something new would crop up, server would crash, parts would go missing, people would fall ill, floods would block travel, flights would be cancelled, strike in the city would hits people's movement, etc. They said that there was no way; they could do anything about it.

Yes, they admitted "It is a 'probabilistic environment'. We give target date to everything just because that is the way everybody does it in the industry." And they also agreed that the longer a project runs, the more would be the uncertainty to deliver it on time.

Of course, they got similar results as everybody else. Every project suffered from uncertainty and everybody kept fighting 24x7 to complete their projects, but got frustrated at the end. Nobody was happy (the least was the client). Some managers were pseudo-happy that teams were working more than scheduled 8 hrs without asking for extra money. They could at least claim that on their part, people worked hard..... But for uncertainty, the projects would have been delivered on time. (There was another aspect, since there were uncertainties, sometime certain features of product were also overlooked and missed)

I had to tell Anthony that *if the project environment is probabilistic in nature then the planning has to 'take care' of probabilistic nature of the project.* And there were techniques that he could use. But I cautioned that implementing the technique without having buy-in of people would not be a good idea.

"What does it means 'to take care of probabilistic nature of the project'?" Anthony had asked.

I said, "Today when projects are planned, they are broken into tasks and then they are sequenced. After this, resources are assigned. Resources are then asked to give time 'ESTIMATION' of their tasks. The time estimations are plugged into the project's critical path and it is thus scheduled."

"The issue here is that 'ESTIMATIONS' are 'ESTIMATIONS'. By definition and design, they are NOT accurate figures. Hence, the due date is never 'deterministic', but people are 'MADE TO COMMIT' to these (inaccurate) estimations. Hence, most of the projects are grossly erroneous at the planning stage itself. It is a different case that people are driven crazy like herds of cattle to meet the due date and they succumb to pressure and work 24x7 instead of planned 8 hrs a day shift; and the project is finished somehow."

"So, what do we do?"

"So, in order to deal with this, it is important that project managers are made to learn to separate out the uncertainties from the overall estimate and deal with them separately than dealing with estimates at each task stage. This is important, since at the task level, people must focus on task and be less worried about the decision making related to logistics."

"By taking actions at planning stage itself, in most cased project cycle time can be cut by 10-25%, while a remarkable and measurable improvement in due date performance is effected."

"Actually, this is not new or out of world approach. In financial management, while making budget, finance managers are asked to aggressively price each item, but account for uncertainty separately."

"Theory of Constraints, TOC gives a way to deal with project uncertainty at planning stage. However, it may not be possible for the project manager to do this, unless there is an understanding, acceptance and behavioral change in the organization. *Most importantly, the organization must be looking out for an ambitious improvement in its performance. TOC is not for everybody!!!*"

171

Anthony seemed to have suddenly found the spark. I then took him to issues beyond planning and explained him how uncertainties are handled in execution stage of the project. I reminded him that TOC has the power to give dramatic improvement but such improvement can't happen unless there is a strong 'buy in' from people and they are ready for a massive cultural change. The strength of TOC is that it connects human element to management techniques.

The day was already stretching longer for me; leaving some TO DO for Anthony, I moved out of the Center. Anthony promised to send presentation of his learning from the discussion, so that he could systematically present a strategy to the Center's head. We had a feeling that perhaps, we run a pilot.

…end…

References

[1] Eliyahu M Goldratt, The Choice, North River Press, 2008

[2] Eliyahu M Goldratt, Book: Goal-The Process of Ongoing Improvement, Third Edition, Great Barrington, MA: North River Press

[3] Eliyahu M Goldratt, Production: The TOC Way, Revised edition, North River Press, 2003

[4] Eliyahu M Goldratt, Critical Chain, The North River Press; 1st edition (January 1, 1997)

[5] Chris McChesney, Sean Covey, and Jim Huling, 4 Disciplines of Execution, Simon and Schuster

[6] Lisa J Scheinkopf, Thinking Process Including S&T Tree, Chapter 25, The Theory of Constraints Handbook, McGraw-Hill Professional; 1 edition (June 10, 2010)

[7] TOCICO, Theory of Constraints International Certification Organization, www.tocico.org

[8] Steven J. Balderstone and Victoria J. Mabi, A Review of Goldratt's Theory of Constraints (TOC) – lessons from the international literature.

[9] The TOC Institute (TOCI), http://www.tocinstitute.org/

[10] Avenir Management Services, http://www.avenirco.com

[11] Goldratt Consulting, http://www.goldrattconsulting.com

[12] Goldratt India, http://www.goldrattindia.com

[13] Mahindra Satyam, www.mahindrasatyam.com

[14] Syncore Group, http://www.syncoregroup.com

[15] Vector Consulting, http://www.vectorconsulting.in

[16] James F Cox III and John G Schleier, Jr., The Theory of Constraints Handbook, McGraw-Hill Professional; 1 edition (June 10, 2010)

[17] Rajeev Athavale, The Echoes of Theory of Constraints (TOC) - Volume 1, an Ebook, LeanPub, https://leanpub.com/echoesoftoc01

[18] Rajeev Athavale, The Echoes of Theory of Constraints (TOC) - Volume 2, an Ebook, LeanPub, https://leanpub.com/echoesoftoc02

[19] James Cox III, TOC Book List, http://goldrattschools.org/pdf/toc-book-listing.pdf

[20] Premlal Yuvaraj, Empowered, an Ebook, Amazon Digital Services, Inc, http://www.amazon.com/Empowered-ebook/dp/B0081HIJG6

[21] Rejeev Athavale, Theory of Constraints - Do It Yourself Kit for Small & Medium Size Enterprises for Manufacturing, an Ebook, LeanPub, https://leanpub.com/tocdiymanufacturing

[22] Shridhar Lolla, The Path - Leveraging Operations in a Complex and Chaotic World, Productivity and Quality Publishing, 2013

[23] Dave Nave, How To Compare Six Sigma, Lean and the Theory of Constraints, Quality Progress, pp 73-78, American Society for Quality, 2002

About the Author

Shridhar Lolla is a practitioner of Business Model Innovation, Focused Execution and Operational Excellence. He handholds business leaders in creating 'built to transform' organizations.

Shridhar is an engineer by qualification and holds a PhD degree from IIT Delhi, Masters from IT BHU Varanasi and Bachelor degree from MANIT, Bhopal, India.

Early in his career, he worked with ABB, Kirloskar Electric, SIFY and Tecumseh. His longest stint was with ABB, the Swiss power and automation technology leader, where he designed and developed electrical machines and later, he became part of the start-up team that built ABB's Corporate Research Centre in India. As the Head of Applications and Solutions Group, he was responsible for creating R&D programs in Manufacturing, Industrial Automation and Power Technology.

Since then, he has gained extensive experience in achieving breakthrough performance in Engineering, Product Development, R&D, IT Services, Software Development and Manufacturing Industries.

He is an application expert of Theory of Constraints (TOC) and shares his time with Goldratt Consulting in implementing principles of TOC. He also runs Time2Change, an online Hub of Operational Excellence, where practitioners from different industry segments are collaborating to assemble their experience on breakthrough performance.

He is the author of a game changing book, 'The Path - Leveraging Operations in a Complex and Chaotic World'. The Path is a semi business novel that shares real life situation of professionals involved in day to day operations and the way they figure out their own way to create the pathway to excellence.

Shridhar is a recognized coach for first generation entrepreneurs and is a part of Indian entrepreneurship ecosystem.

Spending the day with operational teams and conducting walk through programs is Shridhar's calling. He lives in Bangalore, India.

Connect with Shridhar Lolla Online

Email id: lolla@cvmark.com

Website / Blog: http://cvmark.com
Amazon Author page: amazon.com/author/lolla

Check the Kindle and eBook Version of this book at
http://www.amazon.com/dp/B00CIZR1LQ
http://www.smashwords.com/profile/view/shridharlolla

Also check his game changing partial business novel, co-created
with over 100 practitioners from various industries, 'The Path -
Leveraging Operations in a Complex and Chaotic World'
Print Version : https://www.createspace.com/4194640
Kindle version: http://www.amazon.com/dp/B00BW6LA96
eBook Version: https://www.smashwords.com/books/view/325264

www.ingramcontent.com/pod-product-compliance
Lightning Source LLC
Chambersburg PA
CBHW051213170526
45166CB00005B/1881